War on Terrorism

LEADERS AND GENERALS

Titles in The American War Library series include:

The War on Terrorism
Combating the Global Terrorist Threat
Leaders and Generals
Life of an American Soldier in Afghanistan
The War at Home
The War in Afghanistan
Weapons of War

The American Revolution

The Civil War

The Cold War

The Korean War

The Persian Gulf War

The Vietnam War

World War I

World War II

AMERICAN
WAR LIBRARY

War on Terrorism

LEADERS AND GENERALS

by Diane Yancey

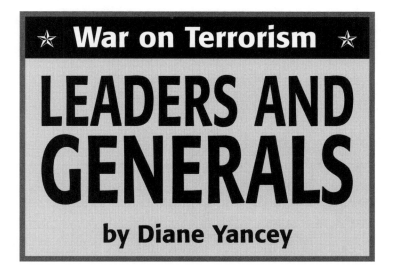

LUCENT
BOOKS®

THOMSON
———✶———
GALE

San Diego • Detroit • New York • San Francisco • Cleveland • New Haven, Conn. • Waterville, Maine • London • Munich

LIBRARY OF CONGRESS CATALOGING-IN-PUBLICATION DATA

Yancey, Diane.
    Leaders and generals / by Diane Yancey.
        v. cm. — (American war library. War on terrorism series)
Includes bibliographical references and index.
Contents: Combatants in the war on terrorism—Most wanted fugitive—Commander in
Chief—Soldier's general—Commander of the faithful—Leader of a broken nation—
Seasoned warrior—Pakistan's risk taker
    ISBN 1-59018-328-2 (hardback : alk. paper)
    1. War on Terrorism, 2001—Biography—Juvenile literature . 2. Heads of state—
Biography—Juvenile literature. 3. Generals—Biography—Juvenile literature. [1. War
on Terrorism, 2001–2. Heads of state. 3. Generals.] I. Title. II. Series
    HV6431.Y35 2003
     973.931'092'2—dc21

                                    2002155393

Printed in the United States of America

★ Contents ★

A Nation Forged by War

The United States, like many nations, was forged and defined by war. Despite Benjamin Franklin's opinion that "There never was a good war or a bad peace," the United States owes its very existence to the War of Independence, one to which Franklin wholeheartedly subscribed. The country forged by war in 1776 was tempered and made stronger by the Civil War in the 1860s.

The Texas Revolution, the Mexican-American War, and the Spanish-American War expanded the country's borders and gave it overseas possessions. These wars made the United States a world power, but this status came with a price, as the nation became a key but reluctant player in both World War I and World War II.

Each successive war further defined the country's role on the world stage. Following World War II, U.S. foreign policy redefined itself to focus on the role of defender, not only of the freedom of its own citizens, but also of the freedom of people everywhere. During the cold war that followed World War II until the collapse of the Soviet Union, defending the world meant fighting communism. This goal, manifested in the Korean and Vietnam conflicts, proved elusive, and soured the American public on its achievability. As the United States emerged as the world's sole superpower, American foreign policy has been guided less by national interest and more by protecting international human rights. But as involvement in Somalia and Kosovo prove, this goal has been equally elusive.

As a result, the country's view of itself changed. Bolstered by victories in World Wars I and II, Americans first relished the role of protector. But, as war followed war in a seemingly endless procession, Americans began to doubt their leaders, their motives, and themselves. The Vietnam War especially caused people to question the validity of sending its young people to die in places where they were not particularly wanted and for people who did not seem especially grateful.

While the most obvious changes brought about by America's wars have been geopolitical in nature, many other aspects of society have been touched. War often does not bring about change directly, but acts instead like the catalyst in a chemical reaction, accelerating changes already in progress.

Some of these changes have been societal. The role of women in the United States had been slowly changing, but World War II put thousands into the workforce and into uniform. They might have gone back to being housewives after the war, but equality, once experienced, would not be forgotten.

Likewise, wars have accelerated technological change. The necessity for faster airplanes and more destructive bombs led to the development of jet planes and nuclear energy. Artificial fibers developed for parachutes in the 1940s were used in clothing of the 1950s.

Lucent Books' American War Library covers key wars in the development of the nation. Each war is covered in several volumes, to allow for more detail, context, and to provide volumes on often neglected subjects, such as the kamikazes of World War II, or the weapons used in the Civil War. As with all Lucent books, notes, annotated bibliographies, and appendixes such as glossaries give students a launching point for further research. In addition, sidebars and archival photographs enhance the text. Together, each volume in The American War Library will aid students in understanding how America's wars have shaped and changed its politics, economics, and society.

Combatants in the War on Terrorism

etween the years 1993 and 2000, U.S. citizens around the world were the targets of a number of sudden, deadly attacks. In February 1993 a bomb exploded in the parking garage of the World Trade Center in New York City, killing six people and injuring over one thousand. On October 3, 1993, attacks against U.S. Army personnel in Mogadishu, Somalia, resulted in the deaths of eighteen soldiers. A June 1996 bomb attack in Saudi Arabia killed nineteen Americans, while the twin bombings of U.S. embassies in Kenya and Tanzania in August 1998 resulted in more than 250 deaths. Finally, on October 12, 2000, a boat packed with explosives rammed the navy destroyer the USS *Cole* during a refueling stop in Aden, killing seventeen sailors, wounding thirty-nine, and leaving the $1 billion warship crippled.

All those attacks were attributed to terrorists—individuals or groups who use violence to convey a message. The sponsor of the terror was a man named Osama bin Laden, a Saudi-born multimillionaire who hated America and all that it stood for. He explained the reason for his hatred in an interview in 1998:

> The call to wage war against America was made because America has spearheaded the crusade against the Islamic nation, sending tens of thousands of its troops to the land of the two Holy Mosques [Saudi Arabia] . . . and its support of the oppressive, corrupt and tyrannical regime that is in control. These are the reasons behind the singling out of America as a target.[1]

America Responds

Although the U.S. government had condemned the attacks of the 1990s, it did not declare war on terrorism until September 12, 2001, one day after nineteen of bin Laden's followers hijacked four airliners and crashed them into the World Trade

Center, the Pentagon, and a field in Pennsylvania. The acts took thousands of innocent lives, destroyed billions of dollars in property, and shook America to its roots.

Bin Laden rejoiced over the destruction, saying, "The values of this Western civilization under the leadership of America have been destroyed. Those awesome symbolic towers that speak of liberty, human rights, and humanity have been destroyed. They have gone up in smoke."[2]

Bin Laden had underestimated American resilience and resolve, however. President George W. Bush would not tolerate the attacks, which were in effect acts of war, and he vowed to track down those responsible. He explained to the United Nations on November 10, 2001, that the war against terrorism would be long and difficult, but promised that, in the end, those who were guilty would be caught. "The people of my country will remember those

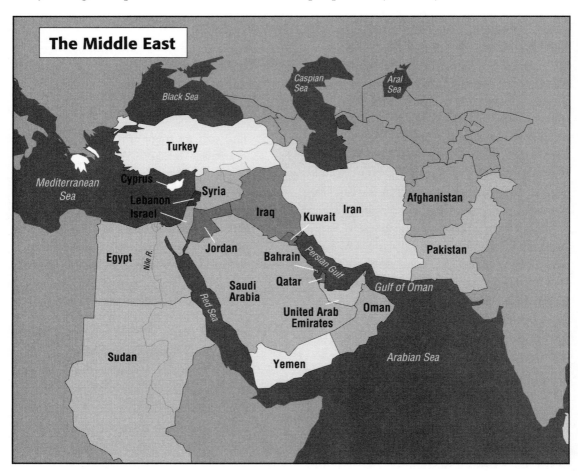

The Middle East

"America Does Not Listen"

On September 19, 2001, Taliban leader Mohammad Omar criticized what he considered America's unfair threat to use force in Afghanistan if he and his forces did not surrender Osama bin Laden. Omar's words are included in an article entitled "Speech by Taliban Leader Mullah Mohammad Omar," published online at the *Boston Herald* site.

> We have not tried to create friction with America. We have had several talks with the present and past American governments and we are ready for more talks.

> We have told America that we have taken all resources from Osama and he cannot contact the outside world. And we have told America that neither the Islamic Emirate of Afghanistan or Osama are involved in the American events. But it is sad that America does not listen to our word.

> America always repeats threats and makes various accusations and now it is threatening military attack. . . . We appeal to the American government to exercise complete patience, and we want America to gather complete information and find the actual culprits.

> We assure the whole world that neither Osama nor anyone else can use the Afghan land against anyone else.

who have plotted against us. We are learning their names. We are coming to know their faces. There is no corner of the Earth distant or dark enough to protect them. However long it takes, their hour of justice will come."[3]

The War Setting

The terrorists that Bush promised to pursue came from various countries throughout the world, but the first chapter of the war was fought in Afghanistan, a remote country located where the Middle East, central Asia, and the Indian subcontinent meet. Bordered on the east and south by Pakistan; on the west by Iran; the north by Turkmenistan, Uzbekistan, and Tajikistan; and on the northeast by China, Afghanistan is nevertheless an isolated region, marked by deserts and harsh, mountainous terrain. Bin Laden was hiding there protected by the mysterious Mullah Mohammad Omar, head of the militant Islamic regime known as the Taliban.

When Omar and the Taliban refused to surrender bin Laden, a coalition of nations that included the United States, Britain, France, and Germany sent military forces and equipment into Afghanistan to work in conjunction with the Northern Alliance, a band of Afghan rebels who opposed the Taliban. Operations began with American planes bombing enemy installations and concentrations of fighters. Ground troops were also inserted both to aid the Northern Alliance and to clean out pockets of resistance. The fighting began in October 2001, and by the end of the year the Taliban regime was powerless. Bin

Laden had disappeared, and an interim government was installed in the country's capital. Bush noted the remarkable progress in his "State of the Union Address" in January 2002:

> In four short months, our nation has . . . rallied a great coalition, captured, arrested, and rid the world of thousands of terrorists, destroyed Afghanistan's terrorist training camps, saved a people from starvation, and freed a country from brutal oppression. . . . The American flag flies again over our embassy in [the capital of] Kabul. Terrorists who once occupied Afghanistan now occupy cells at Guantanamo Bay, Cuba. And terrorist leaders who urged followers to sacrifice their lives are running for their own.[4]

Leading Combatants

In the months following September 11, the world learned that the war on terrorism is constantly changing issues, actors, and locations. It is likely in the future to involve countries such as North Korea, Yemen, and others. For instance, in April 2002 U.S. troops moved against Muslim radicals who attacked Americans and others in the Philippines. Later that year President Bush indicated that Saddam Hussein's menacing regime in Iraq would be the next focus of America's military campaign.

As the fight continues, the world will be bombarded with a host of new names and faces. Some, such as bin Laden, al-Qaeda, and the Taliban, have become familiar. Others, such as the leaders and generals who played significant but less visible roles in the first wave of the struggle in Afghanistan, may be overlooked.

Those who have suffered that fate in the past year include both military men and civilians. Some were elected to leadership and others seized power. A few, like General Tommy Franks, head of U.S. forces, were well prepared for battle. Others, such as Hamid Karzai, interim president of Afghanistan, were caught unprepared and had to rise to the challenge.

Each, however, had his own part to play. Each conducted the war in his own way. All commanded respect from their followers. All will go down in history as heroes or as villains. No matter which, their stories are included here to provide a better understanding of the men who, in the first war of the new millennium, made landmark changes in the nation of Afghanistan and in the vast, complicated reaches of the world.

Chapter 1

Osama bin Laden: Most Wanted Fugitive

The central target of the war in Afghanistan—and in America's broader war against terror—was terrorist mastermind Osama bin Laden, who remained at large in late 2002 despite a massive manhunt that involved multiple nations, spanned the globe, and cost billions of dollars. "Osama bin Laden is the chairman of the holding company [al-Qaeda], and within that holding company are terrorist cells and organizations in dozens of countries around the world, any one of them capable of committing a terrorist act," stated Secretary of State Colin Powell on September 17, 2001. "It's not enough to get one individual, although we'll start with that one individual."[5]

Privileged Childhood

Bin Laden was born in 1957 in Riyadh, Saudi Arabia, the seventeenth of fifty-four children. His father, Mohammad bin Laden, was a self-made man who worked as a laborer when he came to Saudi Arabia

from Yemen in 1930. The elder bin Laden went on to make his fortune as a contractor building palaces for the Saudi royal family. His business, the Bin Laden Construction Group, became one of the largest and most prestigious in Arabia. "He couldn't read or write and signed his name with a cross all his life, but he had an extraordinary intelligence,"[6] noted a French engineer who worked with Mohammad in the 1960s.

Osama's mother, Hamida, was the daughter of a wealthy Syrian trader. She was Mohammad's tenth or eleventh wife. (The elder bin Laden had three permanent Saudi wives; the others came and went over time.) Beautiful and well-educated, Hamida was a socialite who preferred wearing designer pantsuits to the traditional Saudi dress and veil. Despite her beauty, intelligence, and sophistication, however, she was known as "the slave wife" to other members of the family because she was foreign-born. Osama was her only child, and she loved and supported him even when he later turned to terrorism. "I, like all mothers, am satisfied and pleased with my son,"[7] she said in the *New York Post* on December 10, 2001.

Osama bin Laden, who claims to have been named after Osama bin Zeid, a companion of the Muslim holy prophet Muhammad, grew up surrounded by every kind of luxury. His mother had her own home, but he also spent time in his father's palaces. All were large, air-conditioned, and decorated with treasures such as gold statues, ancient tapestries, and Venetian chandeliers. Servants catered to his every need. He and his brothers drove Cadillacs and Rolls-Royces; they traveled to other countries, including those in Europe.

Osama bin Laden, founder and leader of the Islamic extremist group al-Qaeda, is the central target of America's war on terrorism.

One Danish hotel owner remembered tidying their rooms. "They used the extra bed in their rooms to lay out their clothes. They had lots of white silk shirts packaged in cellophane. I think they had a new one for every day—I never saw the dirty ones. They also had a big bag for their jewelry."[8]

Despite their wealthy background bin Laden and his siblings were raised to observe a strict religious and social code. Their father, a devout and conservative Muslim, emphasized the importance of religious observances. He sponsored pilgrimages to the holy cities of Mecca and Medina, and often used his private helicopter to travel to the al-Aqsa mosque in Jerusalem to pray. He always carried a large amount of cash so that he could be ready to help any person in need, and in 1964, when King Saud's mismanagement left the kingdom's treasuries depleted, Mohammad paid all civil servants' wages for six months.

Mohammad not only expected his children to be devout Muslims and good citizens, he demanded that they excel in other areas as well. "The father had a very dominating personality," one observer wrote. "He had a tough discipline and . . . dealt with his children as big men and demanded them to show confidence at a young age."[9]

The children were also expected to do well in school. They were, however, given some choice when it came to colleges and careers. One brother elected to study in England. Another went to universities in Sweden and California. Osama chose to attend King Abdul Aziz University, a publicly funded school in Jeddah. There he studied civil engineering though he graduated in 1981 with a degree in public administration.

Radicalization

During the early years of his life there was no sign that Osama would become a religious radical and a sponsor of terrorism. He was a tall, thin young man who was always soft-spoken, neat, and conscientious in his work. "He was very courteous—more so than any of the others in his class. Physically he was outstanding because he was taller, more handsome and fairer than most of the other boys. He also stood out as he was singularly [exceptionally] gracious and polite, and had a great deal of inner confidence,"[10] remembered one of his teachers.

Bin Laden remained quiet and courteous, but while studying at the university he was exposed to the many Islamic fundamentalists who attended the school. These individuals had anti-Western ideologies and were intolerant of any religion but Islam. Associating with them and listening to sermons by Islamic radical Abdallah Azzam, who spoke of jihads (holy wars), kindled bin Laden's interest in their cause. He became extremely devout, began an intense study of the Koran (the Muslim holy book), and joined in theological debates. He also began to question the cultural changes that were taking place in the Middle East. Many of his people, including his mother, brothers, and sisters, had become Westernized and were abandoning conservative Islamic ideology that decreed they should avoid the contaminating influences of the modern world. These changes troubled him deeply.

Bin Laden's thinking was further influenced by two events. The first was the overthrow of the shah of Iran, and the following establishment of an Islamic republic under the rule of the Ayatollah Ruhollah Khomeini in 1979. This proved that a national state devoted to Islamic fundamentalism was possible, a scenario that appealed to bin Laden. The second event that same year was the seizure of the Sacred Mosque in Mecca by Islamic fundamentalists who allowed themselves to be killed rather than surrender to Saudi government forces. Bin Laden was impressed with their nobility in sacrificing their lives for their cause. "He was inspired by them," observed one friend. "He told me these men were true Muslims and had followed a truth path."[11]

Freedom Fighter

Bin Laden soon had the opportunity to implement his new radical convictions. In 1979, the Soviet Union invaded the Muslim-dominated country of Afghanistan, hoping to expand its Communist regime in Asia. Thousands of Muslim sympathizers from the Middle East rallied to help repel the Soviet invaders. Twenty-three-year-old bin Laden was among them. The cause seemed worth fighting—and even dying—for.

Shortly after his arrival in Afghanistan, bin Laden made a quick trip back to Arabia to raise money to help support the fighting. Some of the money came from his family and from sympathizers, and some was his own. With those funds he returned to establish a base in Peshawar, Pakistan, along the Afghan border, where

Mujahideen freedom fighters rest in the craggy mountains of Afghanistan. The mujahideen resisted the Soviet invasion of their country for ten years.

freedom fighters, known as mujahideen, could gather to get orders and supplies before going into the war. In addition he helped plan and build roads, tunnels, and hideouts for the mujahideen to use. He also set aside money to support the fighters' families at home and helped provide for the sheltering of Afghan refugees in Pakistan.

In addition to fundraising and organizing behind the scenes, bin Laden took part in the actual fighting. Once he joined a force of fifty Arab mujahideen and fought off a heavy assault of Soviet infantry and helicopters. Another time he and his men defended themselves while

surrounded by Soviet troops and bombarded by heavy artillery. "He was right in the thick of it," recalled a senior Afghan commander. "I watched him with his Kalashnikov [assault rifle] in his hand under fire from mortars and the multiple-barreled rocket launchers."[12]

All who saw bin Laden in battle testified that he showed no concern for his own safety and was willing to be martyred for his cause. This was a testament to his growing religious fanaticism. "No, I was never afraid of death," he said in an interview in 1993. "As Muslims, we believe that when we die, we go to heaven. . . . Once I was only 30 metres from the Russians and they were trying to capture me. I was under bombardment but I was so peaceful in my heart that I fell asleep."[13]

In 1988, bin Laden and an associate, Mohammad Atef, founded the movement that would become notorious in future years—al-Qaeda, or "the Base." The organization began simply enough: Its mission was to help document and keep track of the movements of Islamic militants in Afghanistan in order to be able to provide families at home with information on the wounded, missing, and dead. Soon, however, al-Qaeda took a stand—not just against the Soviets but also against all non-Islamic governments. It joined forces with other radical groups such as Egypt's al Jihad, Iran's Hizbollah, Sudan's National Islamic Front, and others. Bin Laden himself became intolerant of even the mildest signs of liberalism and Westernization. For instance, he refused to cooperate with a fellow fighter in battle because the man was clean shaven. (Fundamentalist Muslims believe that men should wear beards in obedience to the prophet Muhammad.)

"A Man Who Knew About Violence"

To bin Laden's satisfaction, demoralized Soviet forces pulled out of Afghanistan in 1989, and bin Laden returned home to Saudi Arabia. Fighting the Soviets had changed him, however. "He came to the jihad [holy war] a well-meaning boy and left a man who knew about violence and its uses and effects,"[14] said one of his former associates. Drawing on that knowledge bin Laden became involved in movements to overthrow the pro–West Saudi government, as well as projects to further the establishment of fundamentalist regimes in other countries.

Saudi leaders did not appreciate bin Laden's subversive work nor his open criticism of their policies. They warned him to stop giving public speeches and holding public meetings. Bin Laden ignored them.

Then, in August 1990, Iraqi leader Saddam Hussein invaded the neighboring nation of Kuwait with the intent to occupy it and control its oil resources. Within hours of the invasion the United Nations Security Council met and condemned the action, demanding that Iraqi troops withdraw. When they did not, a coalition of nations led by the United States launched the Persian Gulf War, which lasted from January 15, 1991, to February 28, 1991. The brief but successful campaign resulted in an Iraqi defeat, although Saddam Hussein was not captured nor removed from power.

As part of its cooperative efforts during the war, the Saudi government gave permission to American military forces to fight the war from bases in Arabia. To bin Laden this was the ultimate betrayal of Islam. From the standpoint of his radical theology, Christians were infidels and the eternal enemies of Muslims. Saudi Arabia was the birthplace of Islam, and he believed that Islamic holy places such as the Sacred Mosque in Mecca and the prophet Muhammad's tomb in Medina were defiled simply by American presence in his country. His hatred of the West increased, and he vowed never to rest until all Westerners were expelled from Arabia and the Middle East.

Bin Laden continued his activities in the Middle East until 1991, when Saudi officials caught him smuggling weapons into the country from Yemen. In response they confiscated his passport and pressured him to leave the country. In 1994 they revoked his citizenship and froze his monetary assets in Arabia. With his four wives, numerous children, and his multimillion-dollar fortune, bin Laden left for the North African nation of Sudan, a country notorious for its support of terrorists. There he financed terrorist camps for radicals from Algeria, Egypt, Palestine, and Tunisia. He also began expanding al-Qaeda in order to better carry out his jihad against the Western world.

Steps to War

According to U.S. intelligence, the explosion on December 29, 1992, of a bomb in a hotel that housed U.S. servicemen in Aden, Yemen, was the first terrorist attack traced to bin Laden and al-Qaeda. Two people, not U.S. soldiers, were killed in the bombing. The two Yemeni Muslim militants who were arrested for the attack had been trained in Afghanistan where bin Laden had established training camps as early as 1986.

The next attacks came in 1993, in New York and Somalia. On February 26, six civilians were killed and a thousand injured when a bomb exploded in the parking garage of the World Trade Center. The mastermind of the incident, Ramzi Ahmed Yousef, was found to have ties to bin Laden. Then in October eighteen U.S. Army Rangers died in an unexpected ambush in the city of Mogadishu as they tried to rescue the crew of a downed Blackhawk helicopter. Bin Laden denied involvement in the first incident but openly expressed pleasure in the latter, stating in a televised interview that the killers were "Arab holy warriors who were [had been] in Afghanistan."[15]

In 1996 bin Laden traveled to Afghanistan and set up his headquarters in the eastern city of Jalālābād, near the Pakistan border. Afghanistan was the perfect setting for his terrorist operations. Many portions of the country were wild and unpopulated. Social systems had been destroyed or impaired by two decades of war. The Taliban, a group of fundamentalist Muslims, had seized political power in 1995 and were sympathetic to bin Laden's cause. They provided shelter and support for him and his associates.

A few months after bin Laden's arrival in Afghanistan, he issued his first anti-American message, a twelve-page fatwa (Islamic religious edict) that encouraged Muslims everywhere to expel "infidels" from the Arabian Peninsula. The document was entitled "Declaration of War Against the Americans Occupying the

"Kill the Americans"

Osama bin Laden's February 23, 1998, edict entitled "Jihad Against Jews and Crusaders" was published under the sponsorship of the World Islamic Front, a group of radical Muslim leaders from Egypt, Pakistan, and Bangladesh. The edict, part of which follows, can be found in its entirety online at Jihad Unspun.

> The ruling to kill the Americans and their allies—civilians and military—is an individual duty for every Muslim who can do it in any country in which it is possible to do it, in order to liberate the al-Aqsa Mosque [in Jerusalem] and the holy mosque [in Mecca] from their grip, and in order for their armies to move out of all the lands of Islam, defeated and unable to threaten any Muslim. This is in accordance with the words of Almighty God, "and fight the pagans all together as they fight you all together," and "fight them until there is no more tumult or oppression, and there prevail justice and faith in God." We, with God's help, call on every Muslim who believes in God and wishes to be rewarded to comply with

God's order to kill the Americans and plunder their money wherever and whenever they find it. We also call on Muslim Ulema [clerics], leaders, youths, and soldiers to launch the raid on Satan's US troops and the devil's supporters allying with them, and to displace those who are behind them so that they may learn a lesson.

Osama bin Laden urges loyal Muslims to kill Americans and their allies.

Careful and Clever

In an article entitled "Osama bin Laden: FAQ," prepared by MSNBC and available on their website, the head of the al-Qaeda network is described as being a painstaking operator who is willing to devote long periods of time to setting up his terrorist attacks.

[Bin Laden's] operations are meticulous, with some plans in the works for months if not years. They are also clever, and bin Laden himself is very much hands-on.

Some examples:

The 1993 World Trade Center bombers cased the twin towers multiple times, looking not just at security but the points under the trade center where an explosion could do the most damage.

The East Africa embassy bombers phoned in credible threats to the embassy and then observed the embassy response.

The 1995 assassination attempt of Egyptian President Hosni Mubarak in Addis Ababa, Ethiopia, was based on surveillance of Mubarak's security arrangements in Ethiopia two years earlier. Similarly, bin Laden operatives videotaped security arrangements at President Clinton's 1994 visit to Manila, knowing he had already committed to visiting the Philippine capital for an Asian-Pacific summit two years later. The tapes were sent to bin Laden, then living in Sudan [with an assassination attempt in mind].

"He may have begun as a venture capitalist for terrorism [willing to take a risk for high returns]," said one high-ranking intelligence officer of his [bin Laden's] evolution as a terrorist. "But there is no doubt now that he is operating like a CEO [chief executive officer]."

Land of the Two Holy Places." In 1998, bin Laden issued a further edict that broadened the thrust of his war. Published on February 23, it called for the killing of *all* Americans and their allies and was issued in the name of the "International Front for Jihad on the Jews and Crusaders," a coalition of Islamic extremist terror organizations that had aligned themselves with bin Laden. These groups included al Jihad, the Islamic group of Egypt; the Jama'at Al-Ulama of Pakistan; and the Jihad Movement of Bangladesh. "Hostility towards America is a religious duty and we hope to be rewarded for it by God,"[16] bin Laden emphasized.

Al-Qaeda

By now al-Qaeda had evolved into an organization made up of two components— a loosely organized group of sympathetic individuals who supported, but operated independently of, bin Laden in up to sixty countries around the globe, and a tightly knit core of trusted associates that remained near bin Laden most of the time. The first group received financial aid, trained in bin Laden's camps, and sometimes agreed to carry out bin Laden's terrorist attacks, but they also planned and carried out independent attacks when and how they saw fit.

The inner core of al-Qaeda was more formidable. It was made up of bin Laden's most trusted lieutenants, termed his *shura al-majlis* or consultative council. Three of these were his sons, Ahmed,

Saad, and Mohammad, the latter of whom served as a personal bodyguard. "With most of the world hunting for him, Osama bin Laden can trust his children,"[17] explained journalist John J. Lumpkin of the Associated Press.

Some or all of bin Laden's trusted associates were also part of the fatwa committee and aided him in preparing and planning devastating attacks on his enemies. These attacks involved a great deal of planning and coordination and could take months or years to be carried out. One example was the bombing of the USS *Cole* in Aden on October 12, 2000. No hard evidence tied bin Laden to the attack, but the targeting of Americans and complexity of the incident made him a number one suspect. Richard Clarke, a U.S. National Security Council adviser, noted, "There are similarities [to bin Laden's style] in the sophistication of the attack, the pre-planning of the attack. . . . This took months to plan, and there are indications of safe houses, and planning, and moving of personnel in. That's a sophisticated attack."[18]

Bin Laden did not usually claim responsibility for the terror but commonly praised the attackers. "The young men rose up for holy war and destroyed a (ship) of injustice,"[19] he said of the *Cole* incident.

Get bin Laden

By 1998, the Western world, including the United States, had come to recognize bin Laden for what he was: a wily and powerful foe who would be likely to use any weapon—traditional, biochemical, and even nuclear—to achieve his aims. That year, in revenge for the embassy attacks and in an attempt to intimidate bin Laden, President Bill Clinton ordered fifty U.S. cruise missiles to be directed at suspected terrorist training camps in Afghanistan. The camps were in remote locales where attendees were indoctrinated with radical Muslim propaganda, trained to use handguns, machine guns, and rocket launchers, and taught how to construct bombs and carry out assassinations and kidnappings. The missiles caused damage, but bin Laden remained unscathed.

In 1999 FBI director Louis Freeh announced that bin Laden had been charged with murder, conspiracy to commit murder, and with attacks on a federal facility resulting in death. He was added to the agency's Ten Most Wanted list, and a $5 million reward was issued for information leading to his capture. It was the largest amount ever offered for a fugitive.

The attacks and the announcement only served to heighten bin Laden's resolve, however. In a telephone conversation with ABC producer Rahimullah Yousafsai shortly after the strikes on his camps in Afghanistan, bin Laden said, "The war has just begun. America should await the answer."[20]

The full import of bin Laden's words hit the world on September 11, 2001, when four passenger airliners crashed into the World Trade Center, the Pentagon, and a field outside the town of Shanksville in Pennsylvania. More than three thousand innocent people were killed, and financial losses to New York City alone totaled $95 billion. The hijacked planes were piloted by young Muslim radicals who were willing to sacrifice their lives to carry out jihad against the enemy.

While the nation mourned and tried to recover, U.S. officials quickly identified the hijackers and established links to bin Laden. President George W. Bush stated, during an address at the Pentagon on September 17, 2001, "The focus right now is on Osama bin Laden, no question about it. He's the prime suspect, and his organization. . . . We will not allow ourselves to be terrorized by somebody who thinks they can hit and hide in some cave somewhere."[21]

Within days of the attacks the United States and its allies had declared war on terrorists and any country that harbored them. When Afghanistan's Taliban government refused to cooperate in the search for bin Laden, preparations were made for war against them and al-Qaeda. The first U.S. air attacks against bin Laden's training camps and Taliban military installations began on October 7, 2001. Forces also focused on possible locations where terrorists could be hiding, including bunkers and caves in southern Afghanistan that had been constructed and equipped during the war with the Soviets.

The ruins of the World Trade Center smolder after the terrorist attacks of September 11, 2001. U.S. officials identified Osama bin Laden and al-Qaeda as the organizers of the attacks.

Afghanistan's Caves

In a November 21, 2001, article entitled "Digging Out Bin Laden," published online by the *Arizona Daily Star*, journalist Sally Buzbee gives background on the caves to which bin Laden fled when America declared war on him and his al-Qaeda forces.

> Afghanistan's mountains are filled with thousands of natural caves, most created by water coursing over limestone. In ancient times, farmers in eastern and southern Afghanistan built a network of underground irrigation trenches called a karez. The deepest shaft, high on a hill, intersected with the water table underground. Water traveled down through tunnels to farm fields on lower desert plains. Villagers also hid inside the tunnels during invasions.
>
> During the Soviet occupation, Afghan fighters dug caves in the shafts' sides to hide weapons and people. And Osama bin Laden spent millions to create a network of crisscrossing tunnels and fortified underground bunkers. Some of the bunkers have power supplies and several escape routes, and they are large enough to hide weapons or even vehicles, said John F. Shroder Jr., a geology professor at the University of Nebraska in Omaha, who studied Afghanistan's caves until 1978.

Osama on the Run

As the fighting continued and intensified, only bin Laden and his closest associates knew his whereabouts. There were unconfirmed sightings of him in the Tora Bora region, an area of fortified caves near Jalālābād, but he reportedly moved locations at least twice a week and was always careful when communicating with his men by cell phone in order to avoid having his calls intercepted and traced. In March 2001 he appeared publicly at his son's wedding in Kandahar. He made televised comments on October 7, November 3, and December 26, 2001, but all the broadcasts had been pretaped, and there was no way to positively identify his location.

In the December broadcast bin Laden appeared gaunt, unwell, and did not use his left hand (he is left-handed) or move his left side throughout the entire broadcast. This led analysts to speculate that he had been injured or was extremely ill. They knew that he suffered from an enlarged heart and chronic low blood pressure and traveled with a physician at all times. They also speculated that he could be suffering from diabetes or kidney failure, although they could not obtain confirmation of their conjectures. Bin Laden denied all physical problems and when asked about the issue in 1998, replied, "Praise be to God for good health, and the blessings of Islam."[22]

As of late 2002, Osama bin Laden remained an elusive and mysterious figure, deep in hiding and protected by those who support him and his cause. Speculation about his location abounded. One theory alleged that he was hiding in a remote locale in northern Pakistan where there was much sympathy for him and the Taliban. A second theory was that he escaped to Yemen. Some believed he was in Chechnya (in southern Russia) or perhaps in a country likely to harbor radical Islamic groups such as Sudan, Somalia, Egypt, Indonesia, the Philippines, or Morocco. There was also the possibility that bin Laden was dead; in November 2002, however, Aljazeera television broadcasted an audiotaped message alleged to be from him.

In this video still, Osama bin Laden (right) attends the wedding of one of his sons, Mohammed bin Laden (center), in January 2001.

A Continuing Danger

Only time will tell how Osama bin Laden's life story will end. Despite the many obstacles he faces—having no base of operations, losing some of his closest associates to death or capture, and being an international fugitive—he remains wealthy, intelligent, and cunning. "You cannot overestimate the danger this man poses to the United States,"[23] states a senior White House official.

Bin Laden still has many supporters around the globe ready to help him in his work. His determination is also a strength; he is wholly committed to carrying out what he sees as God's work. In his words,

Hostility towards America is a religious duty and we hope to be rewarded for it by God, Praise and Glory be to him. Praise be to God for guiding us to do jihad in his cause. To call us enemy number one or number two doesn't hurt us. What we do care for is to please God, Praise and Glory be to him, by doing jihad in his cause and by liberating Islam's holy places from those wretched cowards.[24]

Chapter 2

George W. Bush: Commander in Chief

When President George W. Bush took office in January 2000, few Americans could have predicted that he would become the credible commander in chief that he is today. It is true that, after a disputed election and two years in office, he remains controversial when it comes to dealing with a shaky economy, failing educational policies, and corporate scandal. Nevertheless, his confidence and resolve as he led his country through a national tragedy and into an unprecedented war against terrorism have been admirable. His wife Laura explains the force that motivated him during the difficult times. "George has a strong sense of purpose. To quote the hymn that inspired his book [autobiography], he believes we all have 'a charge to keep,' a responsibility to use our different gifts to serve a cause greater than self."[25]

"Never . . . Take Life for Granted"

George Walker Bush was born on July 6, 1946, in New Haven, Connecticut, the first child of Barbara Pierce and George Herbert Walker Bush. The family moved to Austin, Texas, before "Little George" was two, and Bush senior began his career in the oil business there. His position as drilling equipment clerk, earning him just $375 a month, was a far cry from the office of President of the United States that he would occupy in 1988.

George W., the first of the Bush's six children, was soon followed by John Ellis ("Jeb"), Neil, Marvin, and Dorothy. Robin, born in 1949, died of leukemia at the age of three, when George was just seven. "I was young enough, and my parents loved me enough, that Robin's death did not traumatize me," he wrote in his autobiography, *A Charge to Keep*. "I guess I learned in a harsh way, at a very early age, never to take life for granted."[26]

As the elder Bush worked his way into more important jobs in the oil business, he was often away from home. George W. admired his father immensely and saw him as having a "huge influence on my life."[27]

He also had great respect for his mother, who was in charge of the family's daily routine. She was capable of handling everything from Little League games to discipline. "They [twelve-year-old George and five-year-old Jeb] would get into big fights, and their mother would wade into the middle of it. . . . Bar [Barbara] would always get in the middle of those fights and bust them up,"[28] a relative remembered.

Barbara also made sure that her children attended school regularly, although George W. was too active and energetic to take much of an interest in class work. He preferred sports and social activities. To ensure that his intelligence and drive were channeled in the right direction, in 1961 his parents sent him to the prestigious Phillips Academy, a preparatory school in Andover, Massachusetts.

The Bush family poses for a portrait in their Austin, Texas, home in 1956. George Walker Bush (left) was the eldest of six children.

The Center of Action

Leaving home and Texas was difficult for George W., but the move proved beneficial. "Andover taught me the power of high standards. I was surrounded by people who were very smart, and that encouraged me to rise to the occasion. . . . I was a solid student, but not a top one,"[29] he remembers.

Although not an academic or a sports star the extroverted young man always seemed to find himself in the center of the action. One of his classmates tried to explain

Valuable Training

George W. Bush was never on active duty in the military, but, as he explains in his autobiography, *A Charge to Keep*, living through the Vietnam War and participating in training in the National Guard gave him insight on how the government and its armed forces should work together in order to win a war.

My time in the Guard taught me the importance of a well-trained and well-equipped military. It gave me respect for the chain of command. It showed me, firsthand, that given proper training and adequate personnel, the military can accomplish its mission. After all, the military took a novice like me and trained me to be a skilled pilot of high-performance jets. I also learned the lesson of Vietnam. Our nation should be slow to engage troops. But when we do so, we must do so with ferocity. We must not go into a conflict unless we go in committed to win. We can never again ask the military to fight a political war. If America's strategic interests are at stake, if diplomacy fails, if no other option will accomplish the objective, the Commander in Chief must define the mission and allow the military to achieve it.

George W. Bush joined the Texas Air National Guard to become a fighter pilot.

his popularity. "He rose to a certain prominence for no ostensible, visible reason. First of all, he was an attractive guy, very handsome, he had a presence to him, he had a cool look. He had a way about him, and he fit easily in. . . . Obviously, he inherited some extraordinary political skills."[30]

Bush graduated from Andover in 1964 and went on get a degree in history from Yale University in 1968. The same year he graduated from Yale he joined the Texas

Air National Guard in order to become a fighter pilot like his father had been in World War II. Because so many young men were being drafted into the war in Vietnam in the late 1960s, the move was criticized by some who believed he was trying to avoid active duty. Bush, however, saw the National Guard as the best and quickest way to learn to fly, and he made the most of the opportunity. "Cockpits of fighter jets are tiny and close, and they force you to learn economy of motion. They also force you to master yourself, mentally, physically, and emotionally. You have to stay calm and think logically."[31] After becoming skilled at flying, Bush and a friend attempted to get into a program which rotated National Guard pilots into Vietnam to relieve active-duty pilots, but they were informed that they did not have enough experience in flying to participate. They did not have a second chance to apply, as the program was phased out shortly thereafter.

"You Work, You Dream"

In addition to spending time flying, Bush attended Harvard Business School and graduated from that institution in 1975. He promptly returned to Texas and, with seventeen thousand dollars, set up Arbusto Energy Company (*arbusto* is Spanish for bush). Bush also decided to run for Congress.

Two years later he met and married Laura Welch, a thoughtful, soft-spoken children's librarian he had dated for just three months. (The two enlarged their family with twin daughters, Barbara and Jenna, born on November 25, 1981.) The couple spent their first year of marriage campaigning hard to win votes in Texas' Nineteenth Congressional District. Despite their efforts Bush lost the election. He observed of the occasion: "Defeat humbles you. You work, you dream, you hope people see it your way, then suddenly it's over and they did not. It's hard not to take a political loss personally. . . . Yet if you believe in the wisdom of the voters, as I do, you get

over the disappointment, accept the verdict, and move on."[32]

Despite the defeat Bush was still drawn to politics, just as his father and his grandfather, Senator Prescott S. Bush of Connecticut, had been. In 1986 and 1987 he worked on his father's presidential campaign as an adviser and speechwriter. In 1991, after the senior Bush won the presidency, George W. moved to Washington, D.C., to work as an adviser on his father's reelection campaign. He remembers the important lessons that working for his father taught him:

> I learned the value of personal diplomacy as I watched my dad build friendships and relationships with foreign leaders that helped improve America's stature in the world. I learned firsthand the importance of surrounding yourself with smart, capable, and loyal people, friends who are not afraid to tell you what they really think and will not abandon ship when the water gets choppy. I learned you must give your senior advisors direct access to the boss, or they become frustrated and disillusioned.[33]

First in Texas, First in the Nation

In 1993, George W. decided that he was once again ready to run for office. This time he set his sights on the governorship of Texas, running on the Republican ticket. After a tough campaign against

Democratic incumbent Ann Richards, he won and triumphantly set about doing his best to fulfill the campaign promises he had made.

Although many segments of the public soon saw him as a competent leader, and his nonconfrontational manner and emphasis on issues such as education and welfare reform made him popular, others were more critical. They pointed to the fact that Texas schools were still failing to adequately educate many students. They criticized his lack of concern for the environment, particularly when he passed laws undermining federal public health standards, state pollution inspections, and regulations on industry. They noted his support for capital punishment and the fact that Texas had become a national leader in executions. They deplored his support of big business at the expense of the poor. In fact, many believed that Bush's motto, "compassionate conservatism," was just another way of expecting underprivileged, uneducated Texans to improve their lives by their own efforts.

Despite the criticism Bush won re-election in 1998 with 69 percent of the vote and became the first Texas governor to be elected to consecutive four-year terms. He later observed, "The election returns showed the people of Texas not only agreed with my agenda but also appreciated my positive, issue-specific campaign."[34]

Bush had proven that he could lead the state of Texas, but when he announced that he was running for the presidency in June 1999, critics insisted that he was too inexperienced in foreign policy to be the leader of the most powerful nation in the world. They believed that Vice President Al Gore, the Democratic candidate, would be better suited for the task. However, Bush's supporters pointed out that George W.'s close association with his father during the senior Bush's presidency had helped prepare him for the challenges of the office. As months passed both candidates gained strong followings, and polls showed the election would be extremely close.

Election day, November 7, 2000, was one of the most unique the nation had ever experienced. Voting irregularities in Florida caused tensions to rise throughout the day. After the polls closed news stations quickly jumped to predict that Gore had won the election—only to cancel their decisions a few hours later and declare Bush the winner. Then, in the middle of the night, they once again modified their statements and declared that the numbers were too close to call. Bush, Gore, and the nation had to wait more than a month and endure endless recounts and several challenges in the Florida courts before the results were known. Finally the case went to the Supreme Court where, after much deliberation, the justices made a decision that put Bush in the White House.

George W. Bush began his presidency on January 20, 2001, under a cloud of division and uncertainty. After the controversy in Florida, many Americans believed he should not be president at all. Others

Al Gore (left) shakes hands with George W. Bush prior to a presidential debate in the 2000 election.

A.M., American Airlines Flight 11 out of Boston, Massachusetts, crashed into the north tower of the World Trade Center, tearing an enormous hole in the building and setting it afire. Less than twenty minutes later a second plane, United Airlines Flight 175 from Boston, crashed into the south tower and exploded.

As the two towers burned and collapsed, American Airlines Flight 77 dove into the Pentagon and United Airlines Flight 93 nose-dived into the Pennsylvania countryside southeast of Pittsburgh. Experts believe that Flight 93, which had been crashed by its passengers in order to thwart the hijackers, had been destined to hit the White House, Camp David (the presidential retreat in Maryland), or the U.S. Capitol building. Everyone on board the four planes was killed. Thousands in the Twin Towers and the Pentagon died as well.

Before long, experts confidently informed the president, who had been speaking at an elementary school in Florida, and the nation that the attacks had been planned and carried out by al-Qaeda, a radical Islamic organization headed by Saudi-born multimillionaire Osama bin Laden. Bin Laden, responsible for bomb attacks on U.S. embassies and the military destroyer USS *Cole* in the

worried that he would not be able to command the allegiance of the country after such a shaky start. Bush, however, was not beset by doubts. He chose his cabinet and top advisers carefully. He was also confident that he would prove capable of leading the nation with dignity and integrity. "I will live and lead by these principles: to advance my convictions with civility, to pursue the public interest with courage, to speak for greater justice and compassion, to call for responsibility and try to live it as well,"[35] he stated in his inaugural address.

Definitive Test

The definitive test of Bush's leadership came only eight months into his administration. On September 11, 2001, at 8:45

1990s, was known to be in hiding in Afghanistan. There the ultraconservative Taliban regime provided him protection and support.

The afternoon of September 11, Bush gave a short message of reassurance to the nation, telling them that all appropriate security measures had been put in place and that the U.S. military was on high alert worldwide. By nightfall the president was back in Washington after having spent the day consulting with military personnel and national security advisers in various secret locales throughout the United States. Not since Franklin Delano Roosevelt coped with the Japanese strike on Pearl Harbor on December 7, 1941, had a president been faced with such a staggering blow to the nation. Nevertheless, Bush showed no sign of hesitancy or indecisiveness. His remarks that day reflected his resolve. "Make no mistake, the United States will hunt down and punish those responsible for these cowardly acts. These acts shattered steel, but they cannot dent the steel of American resolve."[36]

A Lengthy Campaign

On September 12, Bush and his top advisers began formulating plans for hunting down those responsible for the attacks.

President Bush greets rescue workers at the World Trade Center. Bush launched the war against terrorism almost immediately following the attacks.

"Freedom Itself Is Under Attack"

In an address to Congress and the nation on September 20, 2001, George W. Bush spoke words of comfort and encouragement as he promised to eradicate terrorism from the world. His entire speech, entitled "Address to a Joint Session of Congress and the American People," can be found at the White House's website.

> On September the 11th, enemies of freedom committed an act of war against our country. Americans have known wars—but for the past 136 years, they have been wars on foreign soil, except for one Sunday in 1941. Americans have known the casualties of war—but not at the center of a great city on a peaceful morning. Americans have known surprise attacks—but never before on thousands of civilians. All of this was brought upon us in a single day—and night fell on a different world, a world where freedom itself is under attack.
>
> Americans have many questions tonight. Americans are asking: Who attacked our country? The evidence we have gathered all points to a collection of loosely affiliated terrorist organizations known as al Qaeda. They are the same murderers indicted for bombing American embassies in Tanzania and Kenya, and responsible for bombing the USS *Cole*.
>
> Al Qaeda is to terror what the mafia is to crime. But its goal is not making money; its goal is remaking the world—and imposing its radical beliefs on people everywhere. . . . Our war on terror begins with al Qaeda, but it does not end there. It will not end until every terrorist group of global reach has been found, stopped and defeated. . . .
>
> I will not forget this wound to our country or those who inflicted it. I will not yield; I will not rest; I will not relent in waging this struggle for freedom and security for the American people.
>
> The course of this conflict is not known, yet its outcome is certain.

From the beginning Bush emphasized that the enemy was not a single nation but a network of global terrorists who wanted to intimidate and destroy anyone who did not conform to their fundamental Muslim beliefs. Thus the war on terrorism would not be a conventional war. He stated,

> Americans should not expect one battle, but a lengthy campaign, unlike any other we have ever seen. It may include dramatic strikes, visible on TV, and covert operations, secret even in success. We will starve terrorists of funding, turn them one against another, drive them from place to place, until there is no refuge or no rest. And we will pursue nations that provide aid or safe haven to terrorism.[37]

Bush was convinced that a necessary first step in the war was the creation of a coalition of nations who were willing to oppose terror. The war could be successful only if other countries refused to harbor terrorists and used their military and law enforcement personnel to help catch and convict them. Thus, in the weeks after

September 11, the president encouraged members of the United Nations, the North Atlantic Treaty Organization (an alliance of twelve independent nations committed to each other's defense), and the Organization of American States (thirty-four Latin American nations) to pursue the terrorists as well. Each nation was encouraged to participate according to its circumstances. Some promised military equipment and personnel. Some provided the use of bases or granted the right to fly over their land. Some offered financial aid. Others vowed that they would direct their intelligence agencies to identify and break up terrorist cells.

A necessary second step involved money. If terrorists were no longer able to get funds to finance their schemes, their power would be radically decreased. To this end Bush encouraged the appropriate agencies in America and other countries to deny terrorist groups access to international financial systems, to block their efforts to raise funds, and to disrupt their financing networks. For instance, when information revealed that certain charitable organizations, such as Benevolence International Foundation and the Holy Land Foundation for Relief and Development, were being used to channel money to al-Qaeda and other terrorist groups, their assets were seized.

Streamlining the Military

Bush left the most dramatic and visible part of the war—the military response—

to Commander Tommy Franks, Secretary of Defense Donald Rumsfeld, and other military experts, but he did demand that the military take significant steps to be able to fight a new kind of war more efficiently and effectively. For instance, he asked that they be ready to prevent attacks, rather than just respond to them. He directed that they consider how to best protect American telecommunications, computer systems, and other information networks, rather than just protecting American territory as they had in the past. "[Bush gave commanders] the freedom to make mistakes, to try things . . . and [to] know that your boss is going to let you make the mistakes and pick yourself up and clean yourself off and get back in the game—huge mind-set differences,"[38] observed General Peter Pace, vice chairman of the Joint Chiefs of Staff.

As a secondary part of the military action Bush also strongly encouraged humanitarian efforts toward Afghan citizens who had suffered for years under the Taliban. This included shipments of food and other supplies as well as reconstruction of buildings damaged in the war with the Soviets. The president did not want to appear to be invading the country and subjugating its citizens. Rather he wanted to work with the Afghan people to reestablish peace and stability, set up a government friendly with the West, and train a military that could defend the nation. "In the struggle ahead, we will act in accordance with American ideals. We're

"Axis of Evil"

In his January 2002 "State of the Union Address," found at the White House's website, President George W. Bush emphasized that Afghanistan would not be his only target in the war on terror. His specific mention of countries that he believed constituted an "axis of evil"—North Korea, Iran, and Iraq—drew worldwide criticism and comment in the days following the speech.

Our . . . goal is to prevent regimes that sponsor terror from threatening America or our friends and allies with weapons of mass destruction. Some of these regimes have been pretty quiet since September the 11th. But we know their true nature. North Korea is a regime arming with missiles and weapons of mass destruction, while starving its citizens.

Iran aggressively pursues these weapons and exports terror, while an unelected few repress the Iranian people's hope for freedom.

Iraq continues to flaunt its hostility toward America and to support terror. The Iraqi regime has plotted to develop anthrax, and nerve gas, and nuclear weapons for over a decade. This is a regime that has already used poison gas to murder thousands of its own citizens—leaving the bodies of mothers huddled over their dead children. This is a regime that agreed to international inspections—then kicked out the inspectors. This is a regime that has something to hide from the civilized world.

States like these, and their terrorist allies, constitute an axis of evil, arming to threaten the peace of the world. By seeking weapons of mass destruction, these regimes pose a grave and growing danger. They could provide these arms to terrorists, giving them the means to match their hatred. They could attack our allies or attempt to blackmail the United States. In any of these cases, the price of indifference would be catastrophic.

offering help and friendship to the Afghan people. It is their Taliban rulers, and the terrorists they harbor, who have much to fear,"[39] he stated in a radio message on October 6, 2001.

Homeland Issues

The war took much of Bush's attention, but he also found time to visit his ranch in Texas and to spend time with his parents, his wife, and his daughters. "Every man needs to know that however high his aspirations may be, however lofty a position he may attain, he will never have a greater duty or a more important title than 'dad,'"[40] he stated regarding the priority he put on family ties.

Bush also made time to address other political issues that were important to him and to the nation. He worked for education reform with the goal of giving local governments more say about how they educate children. In this way Bush felt that many of the nation's failing school systems would be improved. He worked to pass a tax relief plan to help working families. He supported the creation of a patient's bill of rights. As the economy remained weak after September 11 and a series of corporate finance scandals rocked the stock market, Bush also began pushing for an economic stimulus package that would cut taxes, extend unemployment insurance, and encourage investment and job creation. Many Americans were critical of his policies, believing that he was not doing enough, but Bush remained convinced that his administration was on the right track.

In the wake of the September 11 attacks Bush also took steps to improve national security to protect American citizens from further terrorism. He designated this aspect of the government "homeland security" and assigned Pennsylvania governor Tom Ridge to head a new homeland security department. Ridge was, in Bush's words, "a military veteran,

an effective governor, a true patriot and a trusted friend."[41] Ridge's job would be to help coordinate a national plan to safeguard the country against further acts of terrorism. This meant that law enforcement and intelligence agencies would be asked to work together to discover potential terrorists and prevent them from striking. Emphasis was also placed on protecting innocent Muslims and persons of Middle Eastern descent who, in the wake of the September 11 attacks, might be subject to discrimination and violence from American citizens.

Pennsylvania governor Tom Ridge is sworn in as head of the Office of Homeland Security. Bush created the department to improve national security.

"We Will Not Fail"

While Americans at home struggled to reestablish their normal lives following September 11, in Afghanistan the U.S. military and its allies achieved significant success in very short period of time. By mid-March 2002 the Taliban had been removed from power, and the al-Qaeda network in Afghanistan had been broken. Osama bin Laden was still at large, but a new government in Afghanistan had been established, with Hamid Karzai—a moderate, well-liked diplomat—as its head.

Bush extolled this progress in a July 2002 message. "The Afghan people have played a critical role in our joint war against terrorism. The United States greatly appreciates their support in this vital struggle. Working together, our nations have made important progress in defeating terrorism and we have given Afghanistan the hope of a better tomorrow."[42]

Despite the achievements, Bush was not satisfied. He realized that domestic issues were extremely important to Americans, and that if he did not successfully restore domestic prosperity he would likely be defeated in the next presidential election.

Bush also knows that the war against terrorism is far from over and must be pursued. A massive attack against America is possible at any time. Countries such as Iraq, North Korea, and others continue to threaten the world. Organizations such as Egypt's al Jihad, Hamas (an Islamic militant group operating in Israel), and Hizbollah (a Lebanese group of Islamic militants) remain active and dangerous. Even lone terrorists, such as Oklahoma City bomber Timothy McVeigh and Unabomber Theodore Kaczynski, are capable of causing death and destruction.

Bush, with such a heavy responsibility on his shoulders, therefore continues to be unwavering in his efforts to fight terrorism. He asks that citizens remain patient, reminding them that rooting out terrorists worldwide is an enormous challenge. He emphasizes the danger of pacifying or ignoring evildoers. He remains convinced that, although the enemy is stealthy and persistent, Americans are equal to the task of winning the war. As he emphasized in September 2001, "Great harm has been done to us. We have suffered great loss. And in our grief and anger we have found our mission and our moment. . . . Our nation—this generation—will lift a dark threat of violence from our people and our future. We will rally the world to this cause by our efforts, by our courage. We will not tire, we will not falter, and we will not fail."[43]

Chapter 3

Tommy Franks: The "Soldier's General"

hroughout the months that the U.S. military fought the war on terror in Afghanistan, Tommy Franks, head of Central Command (CENTCOM) and the man heading the U.S. military, remained relatively unknown to ordinary Americans. The four-star general was a successful military leader, well loved by his troops and well respected by the president, but he preferred to focus on his responsibilities rather than seek public acclaim. "My purpose is to do my regular job, which is to be sure that we coordinate activities that we have going on in the region,"[44] he explained during a short news conference in October 2001.

"A Very Nice Guy"

Tommy Ray Franks was born on June 17, 1945, in Wynnewood, Oklahoma, a tiny community in the south-central part of the state. His father, Ray, was a construction worker; his mother, Lorene, worked as a seamstress and homemaker. The trio

moved to Midland, Texas, shortly after Tommy was born, and there he grew up as an only child in a middle-class household.

General Tommy Ray Franks is the head of the U.S. Central Command and led U.S. forces in Afghanistan.

"That's for Me!"

Franks felt at home in the army and knew almost from the beginning that he wanted to make it his career. In an article entitled "What I've Learned," from *Esquire* magazine and found on their website, he humorously remembers the time when he experienced the thrill of being a notable in the military ranks.

I went for training at Fort Devins, Massachusetts. One morning I saw my lieutenant cleaning his military gear. He said, "Hey, Franks, I need some cleaning supplies from the store off post." He pitched me his car keys and said, "Would you pick them up for me?" His car had an officer's sticker on the windshield, so the military policeman at the gate saluted the car and I promptly returned his salute. And I said to myself, "By God—that's for me!"

He remembers that his parents were loving and caring, and impressed on him the value of discipline, hard work, and good management. "A lesson my parents taught me is, don't buy [expensive] Montblanc pens and Rolexes [watches] on credit. There are certain things in life you pay cash for. If you're going to have the things that you really don't need but would like to have, get 'em when you can afford 'em."[45]

In the early 1960s, Franks attended Midland Lee High School, where future first lady Laura Bush also went to school. "He was very intelligent, a very nice guy," remembers a fellow student. "I had no idea he'd end up in the military."[46] Although Franks was intelligent, he enjoyed having a good time and did not make classes a top priority. Rather, he loved the outdoors, driving and working on his Mustang convertible, and playing football. It was from a former football coach that he gained another valuable piece of wisdom. "If he said it once, he said it a thousand times while I knew him, he said, 'You never quit,'"[47] Franks remembers.

Vietnam Vet

Franks graduated from high school in 1963 and then went on to the University of Texas in Austin, where football and an active social life again took priority over studying. The war in Vietnam was escalating, however, and young people were beginning to examine their feelings about the conflict. Unlike many young men who rejected the notion of serving in what they believed to be unjust war, Franks decided that the army was the place he wanted to be. "I had absolutely no sense of any responsibility to study anything. My grades were so abysmal for the two years I was there that I simply left and joined the Army."[48] Like others in the military in the 1970s, Franks experienced the widespread public hostility expressed toward servicemen and was grateful when that hostility waned in later decades.

Franks took his military career more seriously than he had taken his earlier education. After joining the Army in 1965, he attended and graduated from the Artillery Officer Candidate School in Fort

Sill, Oklahoma. He got his first combat experience in Vietnam, where he served as a forward observer and fire support officer with the Ninth Infantry Division. He spent much of his time at the front of operations directing fire on the enemy. By the end of his stretch overseas he had earned three Purple Hearts for being wounded in combat and three Bronze Star Medals for heroic service.

Back to School

Franks returned to the United States in 1968 and was soon chosen for the army's Bootstrap Degree Completion Program, which allowed service personnel to complete degree requirements by going to college full-time. In 1969, he enrolled again at the University of Texas (this time in Arlington), and by 1971 had earned a degree in business administration. "I was actually a heckuva student because I was tuned in to what I was trying to do,"[49] he remembers.

Franks was posted to the Pentagon in 1976, where he served as an army inspector general in the investigations division. In 1984 he was chosen to attend the Army War College in Carlisle, Pennsylvania. The institute prepares military, civilian, and international leaders to assume strategic responsibilities in military and national security organizations. The next year Franks also earned a master's degree in public administration at Shippensburg University in Pennsylvania.

Love and Marriage

Franks did not climb the military's rungs of success alone. After serving in Vietnam he met and fell in love with Cathy Carley, a student who was preparing to become a history teacher. Franks remembers that, when he first saw the attractive coed, he thought, "Wow!" The two were married on March 22, 1969, and their only child, Jacqueline, was born in 1971. From the beginning, Franks says, he and Cathy did their best to base their marriage on "self-respect and mutual respect, sharing and caring."[50]

General Franks stands at attention beside Cathy, his wife of more than thirty years, during the singing of the National Anthem.

Franks also tried to make Cathy a partner in all his assignments, and she and Jacqueline traveled with him to Germany when he was stationed there in 1973. Although Franks never shared military secrets with his wife, he often consulted her when he had a problem to solve and relied on her advice when deciding what to do.

Franks's reliance on his wife was only one indication of his determination to be a strong family man. Despite the demands of his job he made time for raising his daughter, spending time with Cathy (they enjoy shopping for antiques), and—later—playing with his grandchildren, who saw him as a fun-loving playmate rather than a tough-talking military man. They called him Pooh, a nickname created by his granddaughter when she was two. "I

have no idea where it came from," says Jacqueline, "but that's what we call him."[51]

The Road to Success

Despite showing a tender side at home, Franks was all business when it came to work. In 1991, he served as an assistant division commander of the First Calvary Division during Operation Desert Storm. There he oversaw tactical units battling from helicopters and on the ground.

His success in the Persian Gulf led to his promotion to commanding general of the Second Infantry Division in Korea in 1995. In 1997, he became commanding general of the Third U.S. Army at Fort McPherson, Georgia. And in 2000 President Bill Clinton awarded him one of the most prestigious military positions in the world, head of CENTCOM.

Women Who Answered the Call to Duty

The United States Central Command (US-CENTCOM) was created by President Ronald Reagan on January 1, 1983, to be the successor to the Rapid Deployment Joint Task Force, a temporary organization created by President Jimmy Carter in 1980. CENTCOM, as it is known, is one of nine unified combatant commands that control U.S. combat forces around the world. Others include the European Command, Pacific Command, Joint Forces Command, Southern Command, Space Command, Special Operations Command, Transportation Command, and Strategic Command. All commands are made up of military forces from two or more services and are organized into regions or categories known as Areas of Responsibility (AOR).

CENTCOM's AOR stretches from the horn of Africa to central Asia.

In the 1990s, CENTCOM became known for its success in the liberation of Kuwait (Operation Desert Storm), under the leadership of General Norman Schwarzkopf, and for humanitarian intervention in Somalia. In the new millennium CENTCOM and its coalition partners continue to confront challenges in the AOR such as enforcing the no-fly zone over southern Iraq (Operation Southern Watch) and combating international terrorism (Operation Enduring Freedom). Other important CENTCOM activities include humanitarian and security assistance programs, and training and education opportunities for military members in AOR nations.

As commander of CENTCOM Franks was responsible for all army, navy, air force, and marine units that operated in an area of the world encompassing twenty-five nations and stretching from northern Africa and the Persian Gulf to southwest Asia. His forces totaled roughly 25,000 soldiers, sailors, airmen, marines, and Coast Guardsmen, between 175 and 200 aircraft, and 30 naval vessels. He reported directly to the secretary of defense, who, in turn, reported to the president of the United States.

Man with a Mission

Franks had been commander of CENTCOM just four months when terrorists bombed the USS *Cole* in Yemen, killing and wounding fifty-six service personnel. The commander flew immediately to Yemen from his headquarters at MacDill Airforce Base in Tampa, Florida. "He knew there was work to be done and he wanted to get on with it,"[52] remembers Cathy Franks. Once on the ground in Yemen, Franks met with Yemeni officials to ensure that relief efforts and an investigation into the bombing went forward quickly and efficiently. He also visited the ship and wounded personnel before returning to the United States to report on what he had learned.

It was a busy, challenging period, but it did not compare to Franks's activities following the attacks on the World Trade Center and the Pentagon on September 11, 2001. From the moment the first plane crashed that day, the general was convinced that Osama bin Laden was responsible and guessed that the president would order a military response. He was correct. "Within an hour, we started our broad planning to respond in some way,"[53] testified Lieutenant General Charles Walk, who was at the Pentagon for meetings on September 11. The ensuing war, which involved planning, coordinating, and leading U.S. military forces into Afghanistan, was Franks's biggest assignment to date.

Franks gave it his undivided attention, working with his advisers and with the Pentagon to formulate a plan of attack on the Taliban, Osama bin Laden, and al-Qaeda terrorist forces. The operation had to be carried out swiftly and efficiently, with the smallest number of casualties to both civilians and U.S. military men and women.

Opening assaults against the Taliban were launched on October 7, just twenty-six days after the attacks in New York and Washington. First came days of shattering air strikes and bombing runs. Then came assaults from U.S. Army Special Forces and U.S. Army Rangers who worked in tandem with the anti-Taliban Northern Alliance. Other U.S. ground forces also went into Afghanistan to conduct operations that ranged from disarming land mines to providing humanitarian aid. Franks's overall strategy involved "event-based" planning—a flexible approach that emphasized progressing as goals were achieved rather than by following a preset schedule. For example, he assigned military forces in

High-Pressure Job

Franks oversaw operations from his Florida headquarters, regularly arriving on the base by 6:30 A.M. and working until 7 P.M. or later. After meeting with his senior staff and getting updates on the war he went to his office, a large room decorated with traditional tribal wedding costumes (gifts he had received on trips to central Asia). His neat, document-covered desk was proof of the large amount of paperwork he dealt with as head of CENTCOM.

Franks's war duties also included daily meetings with representatives from other nations who were part of the anti-terror coalition that President Bush had pulled together. These meetings were usually held at the base in Tampa, in the war room, a chamber about the size of a three-car garage, equipped with a huge oval table and large overhead screens on which maps and military operations could be viewed. Franks regularly shuttled to Washington, D.C., to meet with President Bush and Defense Secretary Donald Rumsfeld. Intermittently he accompanied Rumsfeld to press briefings (meetings with journalists and reporters); his comments were usually brief and to the point. "My business is a secret business,"[54] he stated succinctly on at least one occasion.

Such responsibilities took all of Franks's time and demanded his entire concentration. Nevertheless, his family and

U.S. ground forces in Afghanistan watch for enemy movement. U.S. troops defeated the Taliban in December 2001.

Afghanistan to destroy the Taliban's air defense and early-warning radar systems, directing them to be quick but thorough. Only when the air spaces were safe and clear did Franks move men to another task: destroying tanks and military personnel.

his well-balanced approach to life kept him from feeling overwhelmed. "You simply don't find a release from [the pressure, but] I don't feel overly stressed in the thing. I get enough rest. I get enough exercise. And I have an awful lot of great people who work around me,"[55] he explained.

"These People Are Absolutely Marvelous"

Despite his hectic schedule Franks made time to visit those who were vital to the war effort—the sixty-five hundred American troops who were fighting the war. Not only did he see them as true heroes, he viewed them as his extended family and expressed unshakable confidence in them. "I see in the troops the same thing that I see in the streets of America, and that is honestly a depth of commitment, a depth of resolve, a sense of accomplishment that I have not seen in the thirty-five years that I have worn the uniform. I think these people are absolutely marvelous,"[56] he explained. His wife, who learned from years of experience that her husband would rather be in the field than behind a desk or in front of television cameras, noted, "He is a soldier's general."[57]

The general's confidence in his men and women was reflected in his willingness to trust their judgment when it came time to carry out their missions. He believed that letting those on the ground use their brains and creativity would lead to greater success in the war. "Never [deny] the possibilities when one considers the human spirit—the spirit of men and women in uniform. . . . One of the things we don't want to leave behind as we move toward tomorrow is the ability to think, the ability to adapt,"[58] he emphasized.

The wisdom of trusting in his troops'

All About Freedom

During an interview entitled "A Man and His Mission," published in the *St. Petersburg Times* and available online at their website, Tommy Franks explains that, for him, the purpose of the war is to protect a way of life that is precious to the American people.

[I pray for] the country. The way of life that this country has had since I was a kid growing up. I told an awful lot of people and an awful lot of my troops that what all this is about is a way of life. And, I remember when I was growing up and I had friends, some of them had more money than my family and some of them had less money than my family, but we were all blessed in that we really could be whatever we wanted to be. We could do whatever we wanted to do. And when I have a chance to go to a football game down here and watch the Bucs [Tampa Bay Buccaneers] play, which I just truly enjoyed this past weekend, or when I have a chance to be around people on the streets downtown, what I think about (is) it would really be a terrible thing for America to lose this ability that we had to do anything we want to do, and I don't think we're gonna give that up to terrorism. So what I pray for, what I pray about is our leadership, the people who we put in harm's way every day, thousands of them, that they be cared for. That our kids, our grandkids have the luxury—and it is a luxury—of a way of life we enjoy in this country.

General Franks greets troops at Bagram Air Base in Afghanistan. Throughout the war, the general ensured that his troops were as comfortable as possible.

craft carrier *Theodore Roosevelt* during the 2001 December holidays.

The general also made sure his men and women were well cared for in everything from good food to first-class entertainment. With his support, in January 2002 Burger King began providing troops with Whoppers from mobile kitchens within Afghanistan. And on Christmas Eve 2001 he supported—and attended—a USO (United Services Organization) show for troops stationed in Kandahar, bringing in singer Wayne Newton, comedian Drew Carey, and the Dallas Cowboy cheerleaders to entertain them.

Commendation and Criticism

Those who had known Franks from his youth were not surprised by his competent, commonsense approach to the war. They remembered him as a promising young man and were pleased that he had matured into a person capable of leading a mighty army. "People grow," says retired general Crosbie Saint, who had known Franks for twenty years. "Sometimes they grow in different directions. I think he's grown in a positive mature way. . . . He understands the complexities of what we're about."[60]

good judgment was demonstrated when U.S. Army Special Forces fighters chose to ride Afghan horses rather than drive jeeps or humvees to get to enemy positions. The actions helped them bond with Northern Alliance forces—who offered the horses—and also allowed them to approach their targets with greater stealth.

Franks showed his appreciation of his troops in a number of ways. During visits to Afghanistan he personally thanked as many of them as possible for their service to their nation and for making the world a safer place to live. "There's no place in my life I'd rather be, on account of y'all out here taking care of my grandbabies, and that's what this is about,"[59] he said while visiting troops stationed on the air-

Not everyone had praise for Franks, however. Particularly early in the war, the press and some members of the Pentagon criticized him for what they believed was a too conservative fighting style. Impatient when they did not see quick results, they urged him to become more aggressive in bombing Taliban and al-Qaeda targets, and pressed to know when he would be ready to send ground forces into the country. "He has only asked for more [troops] in small increments," said one official close to the Pentagon. "He thinks that if we have another 20 dead then people will start squawking, whereas, in fact, the reaction [to the deaths of eight men in March 2002] lasted only a couple of days and nobody is even discussing it now."[61]

Franks remained philosophical about the remarks, both good and bad. "It is only those who believe that all of this should be done in two weeks' time or in one month or perhaps in two months who are disappointed,"[62] he stated on November 9, just one month after the war began. His approach was vindicated when, by December 22, 2001, the Taliban regime collapsed and a moderate interim government was put in place in Afghanistan. Loss of life had been kept to a minimum. Only twelve service members had died during that period.

"Only a Matter of Time"

When the first complete year of war against terror drew to a close, Franks felt satisfied that much had been achieved. The power of the enemy in Afghanistan had been broken, and pockets of resistance had been dealt with so that air strikes were no longer constant. Days of continuous, fierce fighting were over. The new national government was functioning, and its president was being protected by U.S. Special Forces. Coalition troops were providing stability in the country, hunting down remaining terrorists, and gathering intelligence to help prevent future attacks in other locales around the world. They were also coordinating humanitarian assistance efforts, helping to rebuild and reestablish schools and hospitals, and training the first members of an Afghan national army.

Like the president, however, Franks knew that the global war against terrorism was far from over. The Taliban had been unseated, but its remnants remained in Afghanistan and Pakistan, ready to reorganize and strike. Osama bin Laden's al-Qaeda organization had been disrupted, but it had not been destroyed. And there were other radical groups in the world that were willing to use terror tactics as well. Franks noted that the military coalition would have to "stay on the objective" until the entire network of terror was crushed. "It's a much larger issue than just Afghanistan,"[63] he noted.

Despite this disclaimer Franks remains convinced that the war can be won. "There is no doubt America will solve this problem of global terrorism," he says.

U.S. soldiers distribute uniforms and equipment to recruits of the Afghan National Army at their training camp in Kabul.

"It's only a matter of time, and I think this country has infinite patience."[64]

He is also confident that Osama bin Laden will be brought to justice. The only question is whether the terrorist mastermind will be alive or dead when he is found. The fugitive is reportedly in poor health, he has vowed not to be taken alive, and coalition forces commonly kill anyone who will not quickly surrender to them.

The issue does not bother Franks unduly. In his typical unruffled style he shrugs off the problem: "Justice to him or him to justice. . . . Either one works well for me."[65]

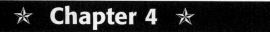

Chapter 4

Mohammad Omar: Commander of the Faithful

One of Tommy Franks's key opponents in the war against terrorism was Taliban leader Mohammad Omar, a man who kept his life largely hidden from his people and the world. Except for time in Pakistan he had never been out of Afghanistan. He had been seen by only two non-Muslims. He had been photographed only once, possibly twice. Even those who lived near his headquarters in the city of Kandahar did not know what he looked like. Some described him as short and powerful. Others claimed that he was six foot, six inches tall, with a long, black beard and a keen, hawklike gaze.

Poor Pashtun

Omar was born in 1959 (some records say 1962) near Deh Rawad in Uruzgan Province north of Kandahar. He and his parents were members of the Pashtun tribe, Afghanistan's largest ethnic group. Even today tribal loyalties in that country are more important than a national government or where one actually lives, so Pashtuns are naturally suspicious of and hostile toward other tribes such as the Tajiks, Hazaras, and Uzbeks.

While Omar was still a boy his family moved to the Uruzgan capital of Tarīn Kowt, twenty miles east of Deh Rawad. His father, a poor tenant farmer, died shortly thereafter, and Omar was left to care for his family. Nothing is known of Omar's early life after that, except for his schooling. At some point he went to Pakistan, where he pursued his studies in several *madrassas* (religious schools) in Karachi and other parts of the country.

The *madrassas* that Omar attended were traditional schools that many young people still attend in Afghanistan and Pakistan. In these schools secular subjects are commonly neglected for the study of sacred ones. Students (known as *taliban,* meaning "seekers after God") are usually taught to read, but then go on to concentrate primarily on Islam and the Koran.

Mohammad Omar was the leader of the repressive Taliban regime in Afghanistan from 1996 until 2001.

Their learning often takes the form of rote memorization of sacred passages, rather than the development of thinking and reasoning skills. One journalist explains, "The average talib, educated in a religious school, can quote passages from the Koran, but it is a good bet that he will not know which countries fought in World War II, that man has landed on the moon, that not all Jews live in Israel."[66]

In the *madrassas* that Omar attended, teachers (known as mullahs, meaning "learned men") impressed students with the need to be extremely strict and conservative in order to live a life that was pleasing to God. For instance, everyone was urged to pray five times a day, live simply,

be modest in appearance, and look upon non-Muslims as infidels. Students who completed their education at a *madrassa* were often not well educated in Western terms, but they were recognized by their communities as mullahs and were qualified to be religious community leaders.

Dedicated to Jihad

Omar had completed school and was working as a mullah when the Soviet Union (USSR), intent upon expanding its sphere of Communist influence, invaded his country in 1979. Pro-Soviet leaders had led Afghanistan since 1973, when King Zahir Shah had been overthrown by his cousin Mohammad Daoud, who declared the country a republic. Daoud was killed in 1978, to be replaced by a new president Noor Mohammad Taraki, who was himself murdered in September 1979.

Upon their takeover of the capital, Kabul, in 1980, the Soviets set up Babrak Karmal, an Afghan leader who had been living in the USSR, as the new leader of Afghanistan. The Afghan people had a strong aversion to outsiders trying to control their country, however, and they began organizing to expel the invaders. It was the beginning of a bloody, ten-year struggle that became known as the Soviet-Afghan War. Despite superior arms and numbers, the Soviets were unable to conquer their southern neighbor. In 1989 they gave up and withdrew.

Those Afghans who fought the Soviets from 1979 to 1989 were called mujahideen, or holy warriors. These were men dedicated to jihad, or holy war, against the invaders, but they usually fought in their own local region. The mujahideen were poorly organized and poorly armed, but their fierceness and willingness to die for their cause made them valiant fighters. They later benefited from military aid from nations like the United States and were helped by mujahideen fighters from other Islamic countries. One of these fighters was Saudi-born Osama bin Laden, who not only raised money for the freedom fighters but also fought alongside them as well.

Mohammad Omar was also a mujahideen. For at least part of the war he served under Mullah Yunus Khalis, an ethnic Pushtan commander from northeastern Afghanistan. Khalis's habit of mixing traditional guerrilla warfare with urban terrorism, murder, and kidnapping proved extremely effective against the Soviet enemy.

Fighting under Khalis, Omar was injured several times. The most serious of his wounds were to his head and right eye, which were hit by shrapnel (fragments of an exploding shell). As a result he lost his eye, and the bits of metal that lodged in his head were never removed. The shrapnel eventually created pressure on his brain, causing seizures, mood swings, and hallucinations; the latter he described as visions from God. "He locks himself away for two or three days at a time and the official line is that he is having visions, but in fact, he is suffering brain seizures,"[67] said a Kandahar doctor who treated Omar after the war.

A Movement Is Born

With the Soviet Union's retreat in 1989, Afghanistan's Communist-affiliated government was left in a weakened condition.

Soviet troops leave Kabul in 1989 after being defeated in the Soviet-Afghan War.

At the same time the country's most powerful mujahideen—so-called warlords with different ethnic, regional, and political backgrounds—began fighting among themselves for control of the country. Rival factions set up roadblocks on main highways and demanded tolls from passersby. In cities like Kabul and Kandahar millions of people fled, and others were afraid to leave their homes as the streets became as dangerous as war zones. Utilities were cut, and food and water became scarce. Lootings, murders, sexual assaults, and drug dealing were rampant, and law enforcement agencies were powerless—or else were in the employ of the warlords. One historian notes, "In one notable incident, two rival commanders in the city [of Kandahar] held a tank duel over a homosexual lover, killing dozens of people in the local bazaar. . . . In another, 31 wedding guests died when a heroin addict went on a rampage."[68]

Mohammad Omar had made his home in southern Afghanistan after the Soviets departed. He had established a small *madrassa* near the village of Sang Hesar in the Kandahar province and preached at a local mosque there. Whether he was aware of the chaotic state of the entire country is unknown, but he undoubtedly understood and deplored the danger in his vicinity.

Two incidents in the spring of 1994 finally caused Omar to take action against the violence. One was, according to him, a vision from God directing him to lead the faithful. The other was the kidnapping of two young girls who were trying to pass a local warlord's checkpoint near Sang Hesar. Hearing that the warlord's men were holding the girls captive, Omar gathered thirty of his fellow Pashtuns to go to the rescue. There was a gunfight, and Omar and his men came out the winners. The girls were freed, and the commander in charge of the kidnapping was hanged.

The incident marked the birth of the Taliban movement, which was originally an organization with a mission to restore peace, to provide security to the wayfarer, and to protect the honor of women. "We were fighting against Muslims who had gone wrong," Omar states. "How could we remain quiet when we could see crimes being committed against women and the poor?"[69]

Taliban Takeover

Details of Omar's actions during the summer of 1994 are sketchy, but by October the Taliban movement had grown to a force of fifteen hundred men. Most of these were young Pashtuns, recruited from *madrassas* along the Pakistan-Afghanistan border, who had been taught a particularly austere and rigid form of Islam. They were not so much concerned about scholarship as they were with waging war on infidels and moderate Muslims, whom they believed were a corrupting influence in the world.

The Taliban was still little known outside of southern Afghanistan. But its

Afghanistan's president Mohammad Najibullah (pictured) was assassinated in 1996 by Mohammad Omar's fighters.

At that point Omar announced that the Taliban was in control and had appointed itself a peacekeeping force chosen by God to unite Afghanistan. He stated that the country would be run under a strict interpretation of *Sharia*, a body of Islamic law that governs all parts of life including religious observances, government, and social and private behavior. *Sharia* would be the only law of the land.

Many Afghans had grave doubts about the Taliban's takeover. Others, however, welcomed its arrival because it promised a restoration of law and order. They saw Omar as a man sent from God and did not even object when, in 1996, Omar claimed the title of caliph (spiritual and political leader of Islam) and Amir-ul Momineen (Commander of the Faithful). The latter was a designation that had not been used since the fourth caliph, Ali bin Abi Talib, had been ruler in the seventh century. Omar also took for himself a cloak reportedly worn by the prophet Muhammad, the founder of Islam, which had been safeguarded in a shrine in Kandahar. To his followers, the title and the cloak elevated Omar to a position just lower than Muhammad himself.

In the role of great spiritual leader Omar was determined to bring the rest of the country under Taliban rule. He sent his fanatical fighters sweeping north, conquering everyone in their path. Kabul, the country's capital in the northwestern part of the country, fell to Omar's fighters on September 26, 1996.

somewhat formidable reputation caused certain northern Pakistani merchants to hire Omar and his men to guard merchandise sent along a dangerous trade route through Afghanistan to Turkmenistan. Omar took on the assignment, but he had ulterior motives that became clear as the convoy he guarded approached Kandahar. When two mujahideen commanders attempted to stop the convoy, Omar and his forces promptly killed them. After hanging the bodies from the cannons of their own tanks, Omar and his men marched into Kandahar and captured it without a fight.

Taliban Massacre

Although Afghans originally hoped that the Taliban would restore peace and stability in the nation, events such as those that occurred in the city of Mazār-e Sharīf dashed those hopes. A November 1998 report by the humanitarian organization Human Rights Watch, and found on their website, describes the extent of Taliban brutality during that time.

On August 8, 1998, Taliban militia forces captured the city of Mazar-i-Sharif in northwest Afghanistan, the only major city controlled by the United Front, the coalition of forces opposed to the Taliban. The fall of Mazar was part of a successful offensive that gave the Taliban control of almost every major city and important significant territory in northern and central Afghanistan. Within the first few hours of seizing control of the city, Taliban troops killed scores of civilians in indiscriminate attacks, shooting noncombatants and suspected combatants alike in residential areas, city streets and markets. Witnesses described it as a "killing frenzy" as the advancing forces shot at "anything that moved." Retreating opposition forces may also have engaged in indiscriminate shooting as they fled the city. Human Rights Watch believes that at least hundreds of civilians were among those killed as the panicked population of Mazar-i-Sharif tried to evade the gunfire or escape the city. . . .

In the absence of a full-scale investigation, there is no way to know precisely how many were killed in the weeks following the fall of Mazar to the Taliban. Based on interviews with survivors and other informed sources, Human Rights Watch believes that at least 2,000 may have been killed in the city and possibly many more.

Shortly after their arrival they shot and killed the country's president, Mohammad Najibullah. "We killed him because he was the murderer of our people,"[70] Omar proclaimed, referring to crimes Najibullah committed during the Soviet occupation.

By 1997 the Taliban controlled two-thirds of the country and had taken to killing rival tribesmen as well as innocent civilians. For instance, in January 1998 they massacred approximately six hundred Uzbek villagers in the western province of Faryab. During the 1998 capture of Mazār-e Sharīf they carried out a systematic search for male members of the ethnic Hazara, Tajik, and Uzbek communities in the city, executed scores of men and boys, and sexually assaulted women and girls.

Innocent Afghans were not the Taliban's only targets, however. They also continued fighting the so-called Northern Alliance, a loose coalition of rebel Afghan leaders who opposed Omar's policies. The Taliban not only boasted more manpower than the rebels but also had powerful weapons, both those that had been left behind by the Soviets and those supplied by supporters in Pakistan. These included aircraft, mortars, rocket-propelled grenades, rockets, and machine guns.

Rigid, Impractical, Controversial

In many regions they conquered the Taliban brought a semblance of peace that was welcome to Afghans after years of war.

Omar soon had a loyal following and was recognized as a powerful figure because he was so pious and had courageously opposed chaos and corruption. The loss of his eye also enhanced his credibility because it proved he had personally sacrificed. "It is our duty to follow Omar, he is our father, the first man to take the cloak of the prophet,"[71] said one man.

Despite his loyal following, Omar and his men soon proved that they had no experience running a government. They were unable, or unwilling, to set up complex administrative, technological, and governmental systems needed to help rebuild the country after war. They were unwilling to ask other countries for aid to combat a three-year drought that pushed parts of the nation into famine.

Instead, decision making was done by a *shura* (council) of Omar's top religious associates—among them Mullah Mohammad Rabbani (who served as deputy commander until his death in April 2001), Mullah Mohammad Hasan Akhund, and Mullah Mohammad Kabir. These men would discuss a matter, then make a determination based on what they felt was God's will. Because of their conservative views their decisions were often rigid, impractical, and highly controversial.

A Taliban official destroys television sets because they are considered frivolous and anti-Islamic.

No Singing, No Dancing

Many laws set up by the Taliban were a result of Omar's so-called visions, which could focus on petty details of life or large social issues. For instance, laughing, singing, dancing, and playing music in public were forbidden. "Useless" activities such as kite flying, chess, marbles, and hobbies such as keeping homing pigeons were also forbidden. The Internet and satellite dishes were banned in order to stop access to vulgar, immoral, and anti-Islamic material.

Standards of behavior and dress were strictly regulated. Men were to wear *shalwar kamees* (loose pants and tunic) and keep their beards at least fist-length below

Public Punishment

The Taliban regime was harsh and inflexible, particularly when it came to those who broke the law. A description of some of the punishments that were inflicted is included in Michael Griffin's book *Reaping the Whirlwind: The Taliban Movement in Afghanistan.*

Despite the emphasis placed by the Taliban on law and order, their judicial procedure was summary [rapid] and non-consultative. Courts, often supervised by illiterate *mullah*, might try a dozen cases in a day in sessions where no provision was made for legal council and where the presumption of innocence was absent. The gravest sentences, moreover, were carried out in public with a clear view to impressing spectators with the terror of the court. In February 1996 in Khost, two Afghans accused of murder were riddled with bullets in front of 20,000 people by the fathers of their victims in accordance with *qisas* [an-eye-for-an-eye justice]. In Herat, a young man was publicly hung from a crane, having confessed to killing two Taliban. Spectators said that he had been clearly

A political enemy is publicly hanged for opposing the Taliban. Under Taliban rule, public executions were frequent.

beaten "close to death" before arriving at the execution spot. In several of the 20 or so reported *hadud* [amputation] cases, hands or feet were summarily axed by Taliban guards without the benefit of a court appearance.

the chin. Western-style haircuts were illegal. Although men had greater freedom than women, they were expected to volunteer to fight the war against the Northern Alliance. Those who hesitated could be rounded up from their homes and taken away. Resistance could be met with death.

Infringement of any laws netted swift and severe punishment. In cities such as Herāt and Kabul, the Office for the Propagation of Virtue and the Prevention of Vice, a religious police force, enforced the restrictions. Any wrongdoer could be immediately beaten or arrested. Thieves had their hands amputated. Murderers were publicly executed. Female adulterers were stoned to death. "Public executions are a big help for the people," claimed the Taliban's foreign minister, Wakil Ahmad Mutawakil, "it provides them with a good lesson."[72]

"The Evil Eye Made Omnipresent"
Some of the first Taliban edicts to be passed were those that enforced conservative

standards of public appearance and behavior for women. Women were classed by Omar as "the evil eye made omnipresent [present everywhere]"[73] and were discouraged from going out in society where they would tempt the male population to sin. If they did go out, they had to have a male escort and wear a *burka*—a robe that covers the entire body including the face, with only a narrow grille of lace over the eyes to allow them to see. "The *burka* costs about US$10," said Zohra Rasekh, a researcher for the Physicians for Human Rights organization, "so most women can't afford them. That's about two months' salary for a doctor."[74]

Because of the expense, many women shared a *burka* and thus had to wait for their turn to go out of the house, even for food or water. Once out they were careful to make no sound as they moved and dared not expose even the tiniest part of

Afghan women ride to market. Under the Taliban, women were forbidden from appearing in public without wearing a burka.

their body. A shuffling foot, a loose strand of hair, or an uncovered ankle could net them a beating or an arrest.

Not surprisingly women were forbidden to work or go to school under the Taliban regime. Women and girls who wanted an education were considered "un-Islamic" and a dishonor to their families. Beginning in September 1996, tens of thousands of women who worked at jobs ranging from secretaries to engineers were fired from their jobs. (The few exceptions were female doctors and health-care workers who were allowed to treat other women.) And, since female teachers were the backbone of the country's education system, most schools closed, depriving even male students of an education.

Worldwide Criticism

In a very short time Omar's hard-line policies drew widespread criticism. Not only did he support violence and violate human rights, he purposefully destroyed historic and cultural artifacts and works of art that the world valued. Of particular note was his decision to demolish the Buddhas of the Bamiyan Valley, giant 175-foot stone figures created in the fifth century. The world saw them as archeological treasures—Omar saw them only as an insult to Islam. "God is one God and these statues are there to be worshipped and that is wrong. They should be destroyed so that they are not worshipped now or in the future,"[75] he said in an edict.

As a result of such blatant intolerance a great many of the country's educated, upper-class people fled Afghanistan in order to pursue a better life. The United Nations refused to recognize the Taliban as a legitimate government of Afghanistan and imposed sanctions—prohibiting the sale of military equipment and freezing some monetary assets in October 1999 and December 2000—in an effort to motivate change.

Even Muslims in other countries refused to accept Omar's title as Amir-ul Momineen and began to doubt that he was the wise leader he claimed to be. They wondered if he could be aware of world events while living such a secluded life. They were also afraid that wealthy, well-educated radicals such as Osama bin Laden—with whom Omar had been friends since 1977—were unduly influencing him.

"No One Can Harm Us"

Despite the fact that Omar's regime drew international criticism, he remained in power in Afghanistan from 1996 until 2001. The September 11, 2001, attack on the United States by Osama bin Laden's al-Qaeda organization drew fresh attention to the Taliban's close links to terrorism.

Because bin Laden was living in Afghanistan at the time of the attacks, President George W. Bush challenged Omar to cooperate with the West and surrender the terrorist mastermind. Omar ignored Bush's demands and his threat that the United States would use force to root out terrorism in Afghanistan. On September 21, 2001, Omar publicly stated, "In terms of worldly affairs, America is very strong. Even if it were twice as strong or twice that, it could not be strong enough to defeat us. We are confident that no one can harm us if God is with us."[76]

Despite Omar's confident predictions, the Taliban—which now included twenty-five to thirty thousand militia—did not come out the victor when U.S. and British air strikes and Northern Alliance ground assaults began in October 2001. Some Taliban forces fought valiantly in towns like Mazār-e Sharīf in the north, but most quickly scattered to safer locales such as Pakistan and the Tora Bora mountains in eastern Afghanistan. Many returned to their own villages where they could blend back into the local population. Omar himself, after declaring that he would "put up a resistance for 20 years or more,"[77] slipped away to an undisclosed location.

In doing so he had to abandon his walled compound outside of Kandahar, which he had occupied with his three or four wives and numerous children. Unknown to ordinary Afghans who had been kept away, the Taliban leader had lived in relative luxury in a home equipped with gold-plated chandeliers, mirrored walls, carpets, air conditioning, and tiled bathrooms. Even in nearby animal barns electric ceiling fans had been installed to cool his cattle. The entire place was a direct contradiction of the simple life Omar had endorsed. "They built this all for the cows,

while our people never had these things,"[78] observed one disillusioned Afghan who went through the compound.

Elusive Fugitive

By the beginning of 2002 Omar's rule in Afghanistan was over. "I hereby determine as of this date that the Taliban controls no territory within Afghanistan,"[79] U.S. deputy secretary of state Richard Armitage said in a statement published in January 30, 2002.

No one knows the exact date that Omar left Kandahar, but he continues to be as elusive as an outlaw as he was while in power. Those who hunt for him believe he may be hiding in Pakistan or in the Uruzgan Province where he was born—and where many ex-Taliban members are willing to shield him. The hunters know that there is little likelihood that Omar and his Taliban regime will regain control of Afghanistan, but the recluse's fanatical conviction that the enemies of Islam must be destroyed make him a dangerous enemy. They remember the words Omar uttered in September 2001:

> I am considering two promises. One is the promise of God, the other is that of [George W.] Bush. The promise of God is that my land is vast. If you start a journey on God's path, you can reside anywhere on this earth and will be protected. . . . The promise of Bush is that there is no place on earth where you can hide that I cannot find you. We will see which one of these two promises is fulfilled.[80]

Chapter 5

Hamid Karzai: Leader of a Broken Nation

Before September 11, 2001, most of the world had not heard of Hamid Karzai (CAR-zi)—diplomat, scholar, and future president of Afghanistan. One American journalist observed, "Some people ask Karzai who?"

"He is the right man at the right time," answered a state department expert after Karzai was nominated to be interim head of the war-torn country in late November 2001. "He bridges the old and the new. He has a modern outlook. . . . He is not a military type, even though he had the guts . . . to try to overthrow the Taliban. So he was not just sitting outside the country."[81]

Distinguished Background

Hamid Karzai was born in Kandahar, Afghanistan, on December 24, 1957. His family included seven sons and one daughter. Little is written about his mother, but his father, Abdul Ahad Karzai, was head of one of southern Afghanistan's most powerful tribes, the Popolzai, who were part of

the country's majority ethnic group, the Pashtuns. Karzai senior, a friend of King Mohammad Zahir Shah, was also chairman of Afghanistan's senate before the king's overthrow in 1973. During Zahir's reign, Afghanistan passed a constitution giving the right to vote to all Afghans and granting women emancipation from traditional Islamic restrictions.

Hamid's family was well-to-do, and he grew up in a big house complete with a courtyard large enough for the boys to ride horses in. In addition to riding, the Karzai family also enjoyed playing cricket and baseball. When it came time for Hamid to go to school he was sent to Kabul, the country's capital. There he attended Habibia High School, an institution that included grades one through twelve. "It was the best. All the high-ranking people of the government graduated from there,"[82] one student remembers.

After graduation Hamid attended Himachal Pradesh University in Shimla, India, where he majored in political science. While there, in obedience to his father's wishes, he boarded for a time at the YMCA. Like other students in the 1970s he grew his hair long and wore bell-bottomed trousers. A moderate Muslim, Hamid had many Hindu friends and enjoyed participating in many social events. In class his intelligence, insight, and good judgment impressed his professors. "If I go back to 1981 and remember his thought and vision, I am confident he will bring peace to Afghanistan,"[83] said one of them.

Director of Operations

Karzai graduated with a master's degree in political science in 1982 and returned to Afghanistan where most young men were fighting a guerrilla war against the Soviet Union. Pro-Soviet leaders had led the country since 1973, but when Soviet troops invaded in 1979, many Afghans rebelled. Known as the Soviet-Afghan War, Afghan efforts to drive out their former allies went on for ten years.

Karzai was an intellectual and a peace-loving man, but he joined the war to liberate his country. Rather than wielding a gun and serving on the front lines, he worked to plan strategy and tactics while serving as director of operations for the Afghan National Liberation Front (ANLF) in its headquarters in Peshawar, Pakistan. "He was mainly involved in logistics, organizing the

mujahedeen to fight,"[84] explains his brother Ahmad Karzai.

Despite superior arms and numbers, the Soviets were unable to conquer their southern neighbor; they eventually gave up and withdrew in 1989. Then, for a brief time, Karzai served as deputy foreign minister in the new Afghan government headed by President Burhanuddin Rabbani, a member of the Tajik tribe and a leading Muslim cleric at Kabul University.

In that position Karzai urged Rabbani to include men and women from all of

Burhanuddin Rabbani (pictured) became president of Afghanistan after Soviet forces withdrew. Hamid Karzai served as deputy foreign minister at the beginning of Rabbani's presidency.

Ethnic Heritage

Many of the divisions in Afghanistan can be traced to ethnic loyalties and hostilities that have developed over time. A description of some of Afghanistan's main ethnic groups is included in Laura King's article in the *Arizona Daily Star*, "Who Are the Afghans? A Look at Ethnic Groups." The article can be found online at the paper's website.

PASHTUNS
A tribal people, with a reputation for being both proud and pitiless. They are Afghanistan's dominant ethnic group, living in large numbers everywhere except a band of territory in the north. Once Pashtun made up nearly half the population; now they are counted by the U.S. Central Intelligence Agency at 38 percent. . . .

Pashtun are almost always Sunni Muslims, the majority sect in the Islamic world. They have their own language, Pashtu, but like many Afghans are often conversant in several dialects. . . . Traditional Pashtun culture has rigid codes of conduct, particularly for matters of honor. A perceived insult can never be laughed off; death is preferable to dishonor.

TAJIKS
The second-largest ethnic group, thought to account for 25 percent of the population. Most speak Farsi. Education and relative affluence, rather than numbers alone, make them a highly influential minority. The Tajiks are native to parts of Afghanistan as well as neighboring Tajikistan, a former Soviet republic. The Afghan Tajiks are scattered around the country, with population pockets in and around Herat, near the Iranian border, near Kabul. Others live in the northeastern mountains. . . . Most Tajiks are Sunni Muslims.

HAZARAS
Thought to be of Mongol or Turkic origin, they have lived in Afghanistan since the 13th century. Unlike other, larger ethnic groups, the Farsi-speaking Hazaras are mainly Shiite Muslims, a minority Islamic sect and the traditional rivals of the Sunnis. Making up an estimated 19 percent of Afghanistan's population, the Hazaras have long been a disadvantaged minority, living mainly in the hardscrabble central highlands.

UZBEKS
Estimated at 6 percent of the population. Uzbeks are mainly Sunni Muslims living in the north of Afghanistan, many of them along the border with the former Soviet republic of Uzbekistan. Between the two world wars, many Uzbeks fled to Afghanistan to escape Soviet repression. Traditionally they are farmers, but these days many are fighters. . . . They speak Uzbek or various Turkic dialects. The Uzbeks' tribal structures, once strong, have loosened, but most Uzbeks' family names are still drawn from their old clan affiliations.

Afghanistan's ethnic groups when filling ministerial positions. He hoped that doing so would help unite factions that were historically hostile to one another. His efforts failed, however, and while watching tribal leaders of the war-torn country divide into squabbling factions, he became convinced that tribalism—loyalty to one's tribe over one's nation—was an obstacle that needed to be overcome if Afghanistan were ever to achieve peace and prosperity. From that time onward he made it a point to identify himself as an Afghan rather than a Pashtun. "The common Afghan man has an Afghan element," he pointed out. "They dress the same all over, they have the same turbans, they have the same clothes, they have the same way of life. It's the problem of interference—it's radicalism that's made our people suffer."[85]

Anti-Taliban

Karzai eventually grew tired of the infighting in Rabbani's government, and, as Mohammad Omar's fundamentalist Taliban regime began to seize power in 1994, he transferred his loyalties to them. At that time the movement was seen as a force for peace and stability in the country. Karzai hoped that they would accomplish what others had been unable to do.

He soon realized that the Taliban tolerated only those Afghans who conformed to their rigid social, religious, and political standards, and he grew disillusioned. He was also suspicious of the large number of radical Muslims from other countries who had allied themselves with the Taliban and seemed to be influencing it. Among these were Osama bin Laden and his al-Qaeda associates. "These Arabs are in Afghanistan to learn to shoot. They learn to shoot on live targets and those live targets are the Afghan people, our children, our women. We want them out,"[86] he explained.

When the Taliban tried to name Karzai as their ambassador to the United Nations, he refused the post. A short time later he publicly denounced them and, fearing for his safety, moved to Quetta, Pakistan. There he began working to build support networks both in Afghanistan and abroad to strengthen opposition to the Taliban. Ahmad Karzai remarks, "All he has ever wanted for Afghanistan has been peace and stability and a broad-based government. He supports [former] king Zahir Shah and he just wants to serve his country."[87]

Karzai's opposition to the Taliban became more personal in 1999, when his father was murdered while walking home from a mosque in Quetta. The elder Karzai had also been outspoken in his criticism of Mohammad Omar's regime, and the family became convinced that one of the radicals was his assassin. "He was killed on the direct orders of Mullah Mohammad Omar," said Ahmad. "He was an old man when they shot him on the way back to his house after evening prayers."[88]

"I'm Asking for Help"

Karzai intensified his anti-Taliban activities after September 11, 2001, when the world declared war on terrorism. As U.S. air strikes began in October, Karzai and another prominent Pashtun, Abdul Haq, slipped into Afghanistan to organize Pashtun resistance. Haq, a close friend, was captured by the Taliban and was immediately executed.

Karzai was more fortunate. Entering the country by motorcycle on October 7, he headed to the village of Shorandam, northeast of the city of Kandahar, where a friend agreed to hide him. From there he made contact with tribal elders and others who were willing to join an anti-Taliban uprising. He also made a plea for international assistance to help rid the country of the radicals and their terrorist friends. "I'm asking for help from the U.S., Europe and Muslim countries to help the Afghan people to regain independence, regain peace and once again live among the nations of the world as a dignified, honourable nation,"[89] he said in a November 2001 telephone interview. The West's assurance of support and weapons was encouraging to him and his men.

A few days after the interview a small group of U.S. Special Forces parachuted into Afghanistan and linked up with Karzai. At about the same time, U.S. troops also landed in the northern part of the country to help Northern Alliance fighters there. With this aid the rebels' fight against the Taliban took on new momentum. Cities that were held by the Taliban were bombed into submission. Men who had hesitated to storm enemy enclaves grew bolder. The Afghans were impressed with American high-tech weapons and air support, and the Americans were impressed with Afghan creative strategy. U.S. Army Commander Captain Jason Amerine, who had been assigned to help Karzai, was astonished with how much the Afghans had already accomplished with only a few guns and a great deal of ingenuity. Amerine noted,

Afghanistan's president Hamid Karzai visits U.S. soldiers at Bagram Air Base. After the terrorist attacks of September 11, 2001, Karzai appealed to the United States to help oust the Taliban.

The biggest tool in his intelligence network was the telephone. He had them spread all over the province with key trusted leaders. So he was able to get word right away of anything going on. . . . He worked the phones constantly. I think one of the biggest concerns that we had was just keeping the batteries powered up for him to use. . . . The satellite telephone was his greatest weapon. Arguably, it was our greatest weapon in the war.[90]

At Home and Abroad

Even with the aid of American forces Karzai and his men faced grave danger as they confronted the enemy. At one point they were surrounded by the Taliban and engaged in a fierce gun battle. Only the timely arrival of U.S. helicopters saved them from capture and death. At another time, Karzai was wounded in a bomb attack that took the lives of several Afghans and Americans. Nevertheless, by early December, Taliban-held Kandahar was under siege, and Karzai was able to begin negotiations with some members of the Taliban who wanted to stop fighting.

While Karzai negotiated the surrender of the city, international mediators met with representatives of several Afghan factions in Bonn, Germany. Their goal was to choose a leader for a new interim government that would be established after the Taliban's overthrow. Leaving the country without leadership for even a few days would invite power struggles and possible civil war between rival warlords.

Finding common ground was difficult. Former president Burhanuddin Rabbani believed that he should resume his presidency. Representatives of the United States and the United Nations supported Karzai.

Another group insisted that King Zahir Shah should return and lead the country. After days of meetings, on December 4, 2001, Karzai was picked to head a thirty-member multi-ethnic administration that would govern Afghanistan for six months beginning on December 22.

Karzai received the news by cell phone just after he had narrowly escaped death from the bomb attack. He remembers the words of a journalist friend: "She said, 'Hamid, we just got the news that you are being chosen as the chairman of the interim administration.' I said, 'OK.' I could not concentrate. My mind was all towards the evacuation of the dead and the wounded and the identification of bodies, and all that."[91]

"We Can Work with Him"

With the war still going on in Afghanistan, and with jealous rival tribesmen and fugitive Taliban fighters seeking to discredit the new government, some members of the world community doubted that Hamid Karzai could lead the country through one of the most challenging and dangerous periods in its history. Their fears were calmed when they reviewed Karzai's qualifications, however. Not only was he a moderate Muslim who had played a leading role in overthrowing the Taliban, but he represented the largest ethnic group in the nation, had close ties with the still-popular King Zahir, and expressed willingness to share power with other ethnic leaders.

U.S. secretary of defense Donald H. Rumsfeld accompanies President Karzai into the Pentagon in February 2002. Karzai is known for maintaining good foreign relations.

He was smart—an intellectual who could speak six languages including Pashto, Dari, Uzbek, Hindi, French, and English—yet he was also a man of the people. He even enjoyed the national sport of *buzkashi*, a tumultuous game in which horsemen battle for possession of a headless calf. Most importantly, however, he had political experience, had traveled widely, and stood in good repute with other countries including Pakistan, an unpredictable neighbor. "He is a man we can do business with," observed one Pakistani intelligence officer. "Though he has been critical of Pakistan in the past, we believe we can work with him."[92]

Karzai's appearance and manner also helped fit him for leadership in a modern world. Tall, slender, and dignified, with a carefully trimmed beard and mustache, he had an aura of elegance and nobility that was impressive. The well-tailored suits and attractive Afghan garments that he wore added to the effect. In fact, he was so stylish that in January 2002 designer Tom Ford of the famed Gucci clothing line was impressed enough to name him "the chicest man on the planet today."[93]

Some observers believed that Karzai's clothing was, in fact, more than just a personal fashion preference. They maintain that his choice of both Western suits and

Afghan robes sent a message—that he accepted the West and yet maintained a sense of pride in his own country. Akbar Ahmed, professor of Islamic studies at American University in Washington, D.C., made another point: "With his dress, he wants to revive the best of Afghan culture."[94]

President Karzai

On December 22, 2001, Karzai was sworn in as president at the interior ministry in Kabul, closely guarded by Afghan soldiers and British Royal Marines. At the ceremony Karzai spoke directly to his people: "The significance of this day in Afghan history really depends on what happens in the future. If we deliver, this will be a great day. If we don't deliver, this will go into oblivion."[95]

Taking his responsibilities seriously Karzai immediately began the difficult task of stabilizing his country, uniting the ministers of his interim government—some of whom were longtime enemies—and preparing for a June 2002 *loya jirga* (a traditional Afghan decision-making council) where a more permanent government would be elected. Karzai wanted this council to be all-inclusive—made up of nomads, refugees, academics, religious scholars, and women, as well as an elected representative from each region. Only criminals, Taliban members, and those suspected of being involved in terrorism would be excluded.

At the same time that he dealt with internal affairs Karzai and some of his associates, including Foreign Minister Abdullah Abdullah and Defense Minister Mohammad Fahim, traveled extensively to other countries. Their goals were to establish relationships with, and bolster support from, other world leaders. Karzai himself made trips to Iran, Pakistan, India, China, Japan, and Russia, as well as Germany, Britain, and the United States. There he met with President George W. Bush, visited the site of the World Trade Center attacks in New York, and spoke with former Afghan citizens who had fled their country in the 1980s and 1990s. He pleaded with them to return to Afghanistan and help rebuild it. "You are the ones who are trained. You are the ones who are academics. You are the ones who have professional training. Come back to your country, and we will welcome you,"[96] he said.

To Karzai's satisfaction some expatriates (exiles) did indeed return to Afghanistan. He was also pleased that the *loya jirga* successfully took place in Kabul in June. During the gathering a majority of the fifteen hundred delegates elected Karzai transitional president for a term of eighteen additional months while a new constitution was being written. True to his beliefs that the government should include a variety of ethnic groups, Karzai chose five vice presidents from four tribes—Karim Khalili, a Hazara; Mohammad Fahim, a Tajik; Namatullah Sharani, an Uzbek; and Hedayat Amin Arsala and Abdul Qadir, both Pashtuns. (Abdul Qadir was murdered by unknown assassins on

July 6, 2002, and was replaced by his older brother Din Mohammad.) Karzai also made a point of choosing two women to serve in his cabinet.

He then went to work rebuilding his country. To the best of his abilities he continued to curb tribalism and encourage compromise between adversaries. He pushed for the reestablishment of schools. He worked with the United States to build a national army that could defend Afghanistan from its enemies. He banned the traditional cultivation of poppies

grown to produce heroin and opium, and he encouraged farmers to plant crops such as cotton and wheat instead. Realizing that a poppy crop was a lucrative commodity that some poor landowners found hard to abandon, Karzai offered to compensate those who suffered financial losses.

"From any perspective you look: from the perspective of religion, from the perspective of the country's national interest, from the perspective of the country's agriculture, Afghanistan must end poppy production . . . and we have received aid from international organizations to pay the farmers $250 per quarter-hectare [not to plant poppies],"[97] he said.

President Karzai addresses reporters from his palace in Kabul. Karzai is working hard to rebuild Afghanistan after the fall of the Taliban.

In January 2002 Karzai signed into law the Declaration of Essential Rights of Afghan Women, which guaranteed equality between the sexes: equal protection under the law, equal right to education, freedom of movement, freedom of speech and political participation, and freedom to abandon the *burka*. Many Afghan women, particularly those in rural areas, were hesitant to take advantage of these rights, but at least a first step had been taken. "Patriarchy [domination by men] has existed for thousands of years in Afghanistan," says Zieba Shorish-Shamley, executive director for the Women's Alliance for Peace and Human Rights in Afghanistan. "As we reconstruct the country, we are also restructuring the society. If we don't push now, we will not get anywhere."[98]

Supportive Family

With so many responsibilities Karzai had little time for leisure. Nevertheless, he made time for family, especially his wife, Zinat, whom he had married shortly before his mother's death in 1999. Zinat is an Afghan, but, like Karzai, she has many relatives living in the United States. She is also well educated. As an obstetrician-gynecologist she has worked with refugees in Quetta while her husband lived in Pakistan.

After Karzai set up his government in Kabul, his wife joined him there. For security reasons and out of deference for Muslim tradition, however, she did not often appear in public. But her seclusion did not change the fact that, like her husband, she was a strong supporter of women's rights. "All the Afghan people, especially women, suffered under the Taliban," she states. "Personally, I will try to pursue this policy of improving women's rights in Afghanistan. Education for women, work for women—they are part of society."[99]

In addition to sharing life with his wife, Karzai also found time to keep in touch with his brothers and sisters. Most had fled to the United States during the Soviet occupation of the 1980s and from there had continually provided advice, encouragement, and funds for his political activities. One brother was a professor at the University of Maryland. One taught genetic engineering at Massachusetts Institute of Technology. Two others owned and operated a chain of restaurants, called Helmand, in Baltimore, Boston, and San Francisco.

One of Karzai's brothers worked side by side with him in Afghanistan. Qayam Karzai, who had lived thirty years in the United States, flew to Afghanistan shortly after the fall of the Taliban to serve as an assistant and unofficial adviser to his brother. Qayum was well qualified to be a political guide—he had worked for years in Washington, D.C., to call attention to Afghanistan's troubles, and he was familiar with politics and government. Besides advising the president, Qayum also worked to set up a vocational school in

Afghanistan near Tarīn Kowt and tried to forge ties between that city and Baltimore.

Future Challenges

Despite the support of his family, the Afghan people, and Western countries like the United States, Hamid Karzai continues to face a multitude of daunting threats and challenges as president of Afghanistan. Warlords (local rulers with a military following), regionalism, and ethnic hostility still hinder the country's progress. Inexperienced ministers have to learn how to run key ministries such as commerce, transportation, and agriculture. The country is plagued by everything from earthquakes and drought to bombed-out cities and fields full of land mines.

One of the gravest threats to Karzai is that of assassination—by the Taliban, by rival warlords, or by those who oppose a pro-Western government. Many government members have been targeted. On February 14, 2002, Minister of Civil Aviation and Tourism Abdul Rahman was stabbed to death at the Kabul airport. On April 8, Defense Minister Mohammad Fahim narrowly escaped death when his government convoy was attacked. On July 6, Afghan deputy president Haji Abdul Qadir and his driver were killed outside the gates of a government ministry in Kabul. Also in July, an attempt on several government officials' lives was thwarted when a car full of explosives was involved in a traffic accident and confiscated by police.

After the death of Qadir, Karzai surrounded himself with U.S. Special Forces bodyguards rather than trusting his life to members of the Afghan army whose loyalties had not been proven. His American bodyguards saved his life on September 5, 2002. On that day a lone gunman wearing an Afghan army uniform opened fire on Karzai as he attended his brother's wedding in Kandahar. The gunman, who was shot down almost instantly, was later identified as a member of the Taliban. "I've been through this before. . . . I will not stop. I'll continue,"[100] Karzai told reporters, downplaying the danger.

Karzai downplayed assassination attempts, but he was unable to ignore the fact that conducting business was extremely difficult. The government was virtually penniless. The people were poverty-stricken. Hospitals needed medical supplies. Schools lacked everything from pencils to copy machines. There was no money to hire teachers. There was no money to purchase fertilizer and seeds for farmers. Countries that promised monetary aid were slow in following through. And although Karzai continued to seek outside help to rebuild Afghanistan, he had to avoid the appearance of relying solely on foreign money and foreign troops to keep him in power. "The Pashtuns and people of Afghanistan do not like foreigners," explains Milton Bearden, CIA chief of Afghan operations in the 1980s. "If Karzai starts to be seen

Election Day

On June 13, 2002, Hamid Karzai was elected president of Afghanistan in the first free elections in Afghanistan in at least six years. He ran against two opponents: Massouda Jalal, a Tajik woman who lectured in medicine at Kabul University, and Mirmohammed Nedayi, a Pashtun from Jalālābād. In an article titled "Karzai Elected Afghan Head of State," published in the *Washington Times* and available on their website, journalist Pamela Hess gives an overview of the voting process.

Delegates at the *loya jirga* conducted the voting in 16 velvet-draped booths in the main tent on the grounds of the Kabul Polytechnic Institute, beginning around 4 P.M. local time. The ballots carried a picture of the faces of the three candidates, with copies provided by the International Peacekeeping Force, according to a U.N. official. Delegates were instructed to circle the face of the candidate they wanted.

"Please don't circle all three!" exhorted *loya jirga* Chairman Mohammed Ishmael Qasemyar.

Some ballots were thrown out because more than one face was circled.

Around the large tent, beaming delegates made a big show of casting their ballots for the head of state; some videotaped other delegates with handheld camcorders to capture the historic occasion.

"It's the first time ever in our history that we are witnessing such a situation. I like watching people line up to vote," said Aktar Mohammed, a Pashtun from Ghazni.

as an American puppet put in there by a foreign power, watch out."[101]

Despite the difficulties and the dangers Karzai is proud that Afghanistan is a more peaceful and secure nation than it was in late 2001. Remnants of the Taliban and al-Qaeda are being rooted out of the country. Greater personal freedom and the promise of a more prosperous future have lifted the spirits of ordinary Afghans who have suffered years of oppression.

Karzai also stands convinced that the monumental task of rebuilding his nation is vital to the world's interests. It will be an epic struggle, one that will take courage, creativity, and the willingness to sacrifice. To fail, however, is unthinkable. He says, "I must be very blunt. If the world does not pay attention to Afghanistan, if it leaves it weak, and basically a country in which one can interfere, all these bad people are coming in [again]. So a strong Afghanistan, a peaceful Afghanistan, is the best guarantee for all."[102]

Chapter 6

Abdul Rashid Dostum: Seasoned Warrior

Abdul Rashid Dostum (DOE-stum), one of America's most controversial allies in the war against terror, has been called a butcher, a traitor, a savior, and a hero. All designations are apparently true. With a dynamic personality, a love of power, and an army to carry out his orders, Dostum is intimidating, especially to his many enemies. Yet the people that he leads in northern Afghanistan claim that he is a caring man who has been misjudged and misunderstood. They insist that, in a country beset by war for twenty years, a good leader must be extremely tough to survive.

Child of the North

Dostum was born in 1954 to Uzbek parents who lived in the desolate north Afghanistan village of Khvajeh do Kuh. Little more than a dirt street and a cluster of mud-baked huts, it is about ninety miles west of Mazār-e Sharīf. There Dostum attended school until the seventh grade, when he left to help his father full-time on the family farm.

Life was difficult in Khvajeh do Kuh, even for children, but Dostum made time for what little entertainment the town offered. His favorite game was *buzkashi*, a violent pastime wherein teams of horsemen attempt to toss the headless carcass of a calf into a circle. One journalist notes, "Buzkashi is the way Afghan boys learn to ride—and it's the way Afghan politics is played: The toughest, meanest, and most brutal player takes the prize."[103]

At the age of sixteen Dostum began working for the Oil and Gas Exploration Enterprise in the natural gas fields near Shibarghan, a town of about twelve thousand inhabitants south of his home. Juzjan Province, in which he lived, was a major producer of oil and natural gas for the Soviet Union at the time.

Dostum also began taking an interest in politics and was recruited as a local leader of the Communist Party. The Soviets had occupied northern Afghanistan in 1979 and were trying to conquer the entire country. Most Afghans resented such aggression, and many factions took part in guerrilla operations against the Soviet army. Dostum, however, was a practical young man and believed that he would be better off allying himself with the bigger, more powerful enemy. In 1980, at the age of twenty-six, he joined the Soviet military, seeing it as one of the few ways he could escape a life of hardship and hard labor in rural Afghanistan.

The Dostum Militia

By 1985, due to his shrewdness and leadership abilities, Dostum had become commander of twenty thousand regular militia forces in northern Afghanistan. Known as the Dostum Militia, this group was mainly comprised of Uzbek tribesmen who were loyal to their leader and their region. Under Dostum's command they helped support President Mohammad Najibullah's pro-Communist government, which had been installed by the Soviets in 1979. Dostum was soon named a general and eventually became the single most powerful military commander under the president. His troops were notorious throughout the country for their ruthless courage on the battlefield and their wildness off of it. Despite the fact that his men earned a reputation for killing innocent citizens and

looting, Dostum was awarded the Hero of the Republic of Afghanistan medal by Najibullah before the president was forced out of office in 1992.

Fighting for the Communists meant that Dostum fought against some of his own people, a fact that did not seem to bother him. These men were the so-called mujahideen (freedom fighters), who were seeking to end Soviet domination in Afghanistan. Then, in 1992, Dostum realized that Najibullah's government was tottering on the brink of defeat. The Soviets had withdrawn from the country in 1989 and were no longer providing Najibullah military support. The mujahideen were gathering strength and gaining control of many parts of the country. With an eye to his own future Dostum gathered up the Soviet weapons he had under his control—

Soviet soldiers scan for mujahideen. When Soviet forces left Afghanistan in 1989, President Najibullah's government was on the verge of collapse.

including several MiG warplanes—and defected from Najibullah's side to join the mujahideen. "In the past I supported (Mohammad) Najibullah. That is when he had the support of our people. Our side is the people's side,"[104] Dostum said in justification of his move.

Government Supporter

In 1991, Najibullah's government fell. In December 1992, the supporters of university professor Burhanuddin Rabbani elected him president of Afghanistan. Dostum and his militia initially supported Rabbani, but when the president failed to offer the northern general a position in the national government, their loyalty faded.

Dostum was not the only one to feel dissatisfied. Rival groups had cooperated to drive out the Soviets, but after achieving that goal former rivalries and feuds reemerged. No one could agree upon a way to come together and share power. As a result of these new disputes deeper divisions opened between former resistance organizations, tribal militias, and political leaders.

Unhappiness over Rabbani's election was a main source of friction, and many people refused to submit to his national government. In some cities mujahideen leaders rebelled and became warlords, controlling the towns with their own armies and using military weapons, if necessary, to fend off anyone who challenged their authority. Kandahar was ruled by Sayed Ahmed Gailani. Ismail Khan was in

control in Herāt. Yunus Khalis and his lieutenant, Haji Abdul Qadir, held Jalālābād, east of Kabul. Even in Kabul Rabbani's own prime minister, Gulbuddin Hekmatyar, opposed the president and threatened to seize power at the first opportunity. Between 1990 and 1996, Kabul was the site of battle after battle as Rabbani fought to retain power.

Dostum took part in the civil war that raged in Kabul, siding with first one side and then another. During the time when he aligned himself with Hekmatyar, Dostum's forces fired rockets on the city and killed thousands of civilians. Also during this period, his troops—dubbed "carpet thieves" because of their evil intentions—became notorious for looting and for the murder and rape of residents. Dostum did little or nothing to curb their activities. "We dislike him . . . because of the number of people he killed in 1994,"[105] remembers one civilian.

Pasha

About 1995, Dostum grew tired of the fighting in Kabul and returned to the north to be nearer to his birthplace, his people, and his family. He consolidated his power in the region around Mazār-e Sharīf, a town of almost 2 million people that sprawled across a dusty plain just south of the mountains of Uzbekistan. To ward off rivals he turned the city into a stronghold guarded by tanks, weapons, and a force of twenty-eight jets supplied by Russia.

In Kabul Dostum had proven himself a brutal military leader and an unpredictable ally, but Mazār-e Sharīf thrived under his benevolent protection. Merchants were encouraged to trade with newly independent countries such as Uzbekistan and Tajikistan to the north, so the city's bazaars were packed with imported goods. Balkh Air, established by Dostum and made up of two British-made jets, flew to destinations in central Asia and the Persian Gulf. Schools and universities opened. Women were encouraged to work and study outside the home. "I think he is a good leader because people here can live as they want," said one female student attending Balkh University, an institution financed by Dostum. "I want knowledge and I want a useful life. I don't want to be forced to stay at home."[106]

Dostum soon came to see himself as the ultimate authority in a region that eventually encompassed six provinces. He expressed his power in several ways. He issued his own currency—money that could be used only in the areas he governed. He flew his own flag—three horizontal stripes of black, red, and green. He made and enforced the region's laws and was a harsh judge of lawbreakers. Criminals were often publicly executed. Some were crushed to death under the tracks of a tank.

Nevertheless, Dostum was popular with the people, who nicknamed him Pasha, a title reserved for men of the highest rank

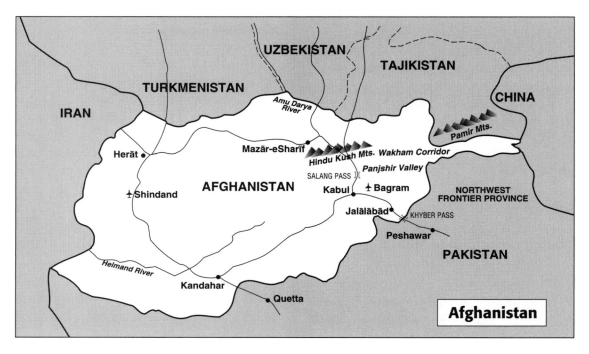

or office. A diplomat in 1997 was quoted as saying: "He thinks of himself as the new Tamerlane,"[107] referring to the great Uzbek empire builder who conquered Afghanistan and controlled vast territory between Iran and China in the fourteenth century.

To Dostum's satisfaction he was even recognized by foreign governments as a powerful and influential person. In 1995, Dostum was invited to Britain and the United States to discuss Afghanistan's oil and gas reserves. He also spoke with Pentagon officials and the deputy secretary of the United Nations, who assured him that the West would support any efforts to oppose the aggressive new Taliban regime that was gaining power in southern Afghanistan. Dostum knew and cared little about the Taliban at the time. "At first I thought, 'Why not let them rule?' Power is not given to anyone forever. If the Taliban can rule successfully, let them."[108]

Change of Heart

Dostum's opinion of the Taliban changed as he learned more about their radical stance on Islam, their oppression of women, and their determination to rule the entire country. Their prohibitions against such innocent pastimes as singing and kite flying, as well as drinking and dressing in Western clothing, were infuriating to him. Dostum was a moderate Muslim who favored wearing an old Soviet army jacket and leather boots, and he refused outright to submit to a regime under which "there will be no whiskey and no music."[109]

In the 1990s, General Abdul Rashid Dostum led his militia in an unsuccessful bid to prevent the Taliban from seizing power.

He soon had to make good on that belief. By late 1996, the Taliban had gained control of Kandahar and Kabul and were moving north. Then, in May 1997, during one of Dostum's absences from Mazār-e Sharīf, one of his senior commanders, General Abdul Malik Pahlawan, betrayed him and allowed the Taliban to take over the city. Dostum was forced to flee to Turkey to escape capture or death. In October 1997, Dostum's militia was able to temporarily oust the Taliban, and Dostum returned to Afghanistan for a short time. In 1998, he fled a second time when Taliban forces again prevailed against his own.

The following months were difficult ones for Dostum and the Uzbek people. The Taliban, composed primarily of Pashtuns, introduced a wave of ethnic cleansing in the north, killing thousands of innocent civilians and forcing thousands more into refugee camps in neighboring countries. Both in the camps and at home, food was in short supply. Disease and exposure took many people's lives.

When Dostum, in Turkey, heard of the hardships, he was filled with frustration. "People demanded that I do something," he recalls. "Commanders, clergymen, women—they would all tell me very bitter stories. I was full of emotions. My friends were struggling against the Taliban and I was sitting there."[110]

"Nothing but Hope"

Such a dynamic person as Dostum had no intention of living in exile forever, so in 2001 he began planning his return to Afghanistan. In 1996, he and two other rebel leaders, Abdul Massoud and Abdul Karim Khalili, had joined forces to form the United Front, or Northern Alliance, to fight the Taliban. The three men and their followers were from different ethnic backgrounds and had even been rivals in the past, but they were held together by their mutual hatred of the Taliban.

After both Dostum and Khalili suffered serious defeats in 1998, Massoud was left as the only opposition leader in the north. He was a tough, determined fighter and had the backing of Iran, Russia, India,

the United States, and other countries. Nevertheless, he lacked the manpower and the weapons to defeat the Taliban singlehandedly.

In the spring of 2001, Dostum contacted Massoud, telling him of his proposed comeback and his plans to gather his supporters and aid the Northern Alliance. As head of the alliance, Massoud agreed to provide Dostum the necessary transportation and weapons. On April 22, Dostum returned to Juzjan Province. "That was when the war against terror began,"[111] he later stated.

Setting up his headquarters in a cave in the hills, Dostum began rounding up those who were willing to fight under his command. This force eventually numbered almost twenty thousand. But even that number was no match for Taliban heavy weapons. So Dostum relied on guerrilla attacks, getting his men from one place to another on horseback, striking quickly, and then retreating under cover of darkness. "They [the Taliban] had tanks, air force and artillery. We fought with nothing but hope,"[112] he remembers.

Grief and Anticipation

Northern Alliance hopes dipped low on September 9, 2001, when two suicide bombers posing as journalists assassinated Massoud. The loss was a heavy setback. One of Massoud's aides, General Mohammad Fahim, was appointed military leader of the anti-Taliban forces, but he lacked the charm and persuasiveness that made Massoud an outstanding figure.

On September 12, 2001, President George W. Bush declared war on Osama bin Laden, al-Qaeda, and the Taliban government who sheltered the terrorists. Just over a month later, on October 25, Abdul Haq, another charismatic mujahideen leader who had been living in exile in Pakistan, was captured (after sneaking into Afghanistan) and hanged by Taliban forces. Haq had hoped to make contact with his fellow tribesmen and some moderate

U.S. military forces prepare to strike a target in Kandahar. U.S. troops joined General Dostum in the effort to oust the Taliban.

members of the Taliban and persuade them to transfer their loyalties to the Northern Alliance. His promised participation had revitalized the alliance, and his death was another stunning blow.

Despite the bleak outlook, Dostum had hope for the future. Convinced that the United States and the Northern Alliance could benefit from working together to break the Taliban's power, Dostum contacted a United Nations representative and laid out a proposal. If he and other Northern Alliance commanders could have American assistance, he explained, the combination of the alliance's knowledge of the country and U.S. mili-

tary might would ensure an easier victory. The United States agreed, and by November 2001 its military was ready for war.

Unconventional Methods

The United States opened the fighting with high tech air strikes, but at about the same time it quietly dropped U.S. special forces troops (Green Berets and U.S. Rangers) into Afghanistan to link up with various Northern Alliance commanders. One of those commanders was Dostum. "Our mission was simple," one soldier remembers. "Support Dostum. If Dostum wants to go to Kabul, you are going with him. If he wants to take over the whole country, do it. . . . It was the most incredibly open mission we have ever done."[113] In the end their participation involved riding horses across the country to sneak up on the enemy and pinpoint his location, calling precision air strikes to weaken him, and going in to finish wiping him out.

The special forces had heard of Dostum's brutal reputation and thus were not surprised when he relied on that reputation for ruthlessness to achieve his ends. For instance, when Dostum heard that a group of Taliban fighters was hiding in a town near Mazār-e Sharif, he went in with his troops and issued an ultimatum to the villagers: Turn over the Taliban and their weapons or the village will be destroyed. The village cooperated.

The Americans were surprised, however, when the warlord was sometimes gentle and forgiving of his enemies. In Kundūz,

"We Need Some Air"

Initially, Adbul Dostum and his men had doubts about the usefulness of U.S. air forces in Afghanistan. The general was impressed and delighted when he got a taste of America's modern military technology, however, as journalist John Hendren of the *Los Angeles Times* points out in "Afghanistan Yields Lessons for Pentagon's Next Targets" (found online at the Global Security site).

> Like most Northern Alliance generals, Abdul Rashid Dostum's experience with Russian bombers during the Soviet invasion of Afghanistan in the 1980s left him skeptical about calling for help from the air. You never knew when—or even where—the bombs would hit.
>
> But on Nov. 8, he had no choice. It had been days since his rebels won their first victory in Mazar-i-Sharif, and he was watching Al-Qaeda fighters amassing to retake the northern city of Kunduz.
>
> "We need some air," he told a young U.S. Air Force special operations lieutenant.
>
> Within 20 minutes, the eyes of Afghanistan's most feared warlord widened as a succession of fireballs erupted over an expanse the size of a football field, killing 259 Al-Qaeda fighters and taking out a command center, artillery and armored vehicles.
>
> "You've got to be kidding," Dostum said. He hadn't expected the strike for a day or more.

where Dostum accepted the surrender of thousands of Taliban soldiers, he assured them that their rights would be respected and the United Nations would deal with them. "When he negotiated the surrenders

Mighty Warlord

Journalist Robert Young Pelton, who has traveled the world visiting war zones and meeting rebel leaders, spent a month in Afghanistan during the war. There he met and got to know General Abdul Dostum. On Pelton's return his impressions of the controversial fighter were captured in the article "Afghan War Eyewitness on Warlords, Future, More," found on the *National Geographic* news website.

I remember thinking how tired he looked, and the next morning when he popped his head out of his compound, there was a huge line of people waiting to talk to him. Every day he spent 12 to 16 hours listening to people, signing things, and making decisions, and I thought to myself this guy doesn't have a name above his door, he doesn't even have a door to put his name on, he's just doing this because it's his natural proclivity [tendency].

He's a very shy man, very gruff, and he looks a little like Bluto from the Popeye cartoons. We kept trying to get him to shave and not wear his grubby old warlord outfit, which consisted of an old Russian field jacket and heavy leather boots. Sometimes he wore a long traditional gown, with a turban and a big belt and I thought my God, he looks like the Jolly Green Giant. We kept telling him he was going to get hammered by the media [press], with a week's worth of stubble and alternating between looking like a warlord and the Jolly Green Giant.

But he doesn't have a suit and the guy who was bringing him two suits had his luggage stolen in Uzbekistan. So much for being a mighty warlord.

in Kunduz, he physically embraced each fighter who came over to pledge allegiance to him,"[114] remembers one Canadian journalist who traveled with Dostum.

Victory at Mazār-e Sharīf

On November 10, 2001, in the first notable victory in the war, Dostum and the special forces with him captured the city of Mazār-e Sharīf. The victory involved heavy American bombing, the killing of hundreds of Taliban troops, and the loss of thirty members of the Northern Alliance. Nevertheless, Dostum was exultant. "We have the airport, we have Mazar, we have everything,"[115] he exclaimed. The capture of the town also meant that the allies could establish a land route to neighboring Tajikistan, bring in supplies more easily, and prepare for a move on Kabul.

After Mazār-e Sharīf, Dostum's efforts turned to the capture of other towns and villages in the north. Each night he would lay out the battle plan for the U.S. forces. "He would say he is going to attack at about 2 P.M., so we would put in for priority for the planes,"[116] explained one Green Beret who helped direct the air war side by side with Northern Alliance fighters. Relatively quickly key towns in the region fell. On November 13, Northern Alliance forces moved into the capital of Kabul, from which Taliban forces had fled the night before. The last Taliban stronghold in the region, Kundūz, fell in late November 2001. Kandahar, in the south, was liberated from the Taliban in early December, and by the end of the year the war was all but over. A new government was ready to be established, and a new spirit of liberation pervaded the country.

A New Role

As a warlord and a soldier, Dostum had played an important part in the war against the Taliban. In December 2001, however, he was asked to take on a more statesman-like role, one for which observers were not sure he was qualified.

International negotiators and prominent Afghans in Bonn, Germany, had chosen a new interim government for Afghanistan, and they had agreed to name a moderate Muslim, Hamid Karzai, as temporary president. Shortly after that,

As an official in President Karzai's government, Dostum hopes to create a unified Afghanistan.

Karzai asked Dostum to be deputy defense minister. It was a position that gave Dostum some power but demanded that he work closely with longtime enemies who had also been given government positions. To make matters worse some of them occupied more prestigious offices than Dostum did.

To everyone's surprise Dostum agreed to the government post and seemed eager to help create a united Afghanistan. Wearing a suit and tie he attended meetings and expressed support for Karzai and the new government. He spoke of the country's diverse ethnic tribes as "its greatest treasure" and traveled around the country counseling villagers to form local governments, take advantage of their new freedom, and get back to work. He also worked to build public enthusiasm for the *loya jirga,* or grand council, which was scheduled for June 2002. "This is the time to set a great example, to build a modern nation that is free, united, peaceful and secure," he stated. "The future belongs to us. We must learn again to trust ourselves, and each other, to build a new Afghanistan."[117]

Justice or Practicality

Many people who were familiar with Dostum's past questioned whether he was truly willing to subordinate his own power for the betterment of the country. They believed Dostum was simply looking out for himself by allying himself to those in power, and they predicted that he would cause trouble in the future.

Some even protested the fact that someone as brutal as Dostum was included in the new government at all. Humanitarian agencies such as Amnesty International believed that the northern general, and others who were linked to atrocities in the past, should be avoided and perhaps brought to trial as criminals.

Those who were trying to reestablish order in Afghanistan took a more practical view of past abuses. They noted that many leaders of the new government had questionable pasts. They pointed out that warlords like Dostum had too much military and popular support to be quickly eliminated. They also noted that, in Dostum's case, he only appeared to want to maintain his power in the north. He was not likely to want to overthrow the central government. Says one Western diplomat, "There are a lot of Afghan people who have done terrible things who we have armed and given money to [during the war against terrorism]. . . . I think it is better to have him [Dostum] in the government so we can try to influence him rather than have him outside to cause more trouble."[118]

Questionable Hero

In June 2002 Dostum took part in the *loya jirga* and restated his loyalty to Karzai, even though this time he was not given an important position in the government. "Dostum said to me he wants to be a hero of peace," Karzai told the gathering. "He said he wants to serve in the interests of peace and fight against bloodshed and guns and work for disarmament. I hold him to that promise."[119]

A new position was later created for Dostum in Karzai's government; he was named as one of five vice presidents and made a member of the National Defense Commission. Because the appointment meant that he had to remain in Kabul, however, he declined it and returned to Mazār-e Sharīf. "I refused to take any official jobs in the capital, because I am needed here. Until safety and security is ensured for all Afghans, I am going to remain here in the North."[120]

The need for good leadership in the northern provinces was certainly apparent. Dostum was faced with rebuilding the region, dealing with concerns regarding inhumane treatment of Taliban prisoners, and encouraging international agencies to continue to provide food and medicine to those in need. In 2002 he also coped with challenges to his power from political rivals, incidents that led to violence in the region. These episodes were a chilling reminder that Dostum's brutal impulses were not entirely eradicated.

Only time will tell if Dostum will be a force for good in Afghanistan or if he will revert to his warlord persona, caring only for holding onto power in his own region. The Afghan government is hopeful that his love of his country will prevail over his self-interest. "I think we all have to live with the realities on the ground in Afghanistan," states foreign minister Abdullah Abdullah. "We have to work together."[121]

Chapter 7

Pervez Musharraf: Pakistan's Risk Taker

As U.S. and Northern Alliance forces fought the war against terrorism in Afghanistan, large numbers of Taliban and al-Qaeda fighters fled east into Pakistan, where Muslims sympathetic to the radical Islamic cause were willing to hide them. The United States needed the cooperation of President Pervez Musharraf (mu-SHAH-rahv), of the Pakistan government, either to allow U.S. troops into the country to continue the fight or to direct the Pakistan military to carry on the fight themselves.

Musharraf's cooperation seemed unlikely. He had supported the Taliban, had seized power in Pakistan during a military coup, and had ruled the country as a quasi dictator for two years. To everyone's relief, however, he proved to be a reasonable and open-minded leader who was ready to risk his own future to aid the United States in its quest to destroy the terrorists.

Descendant of the Prophet

Pervez Musharraf was born on August 11, 1943, in New Delhi, India. His parents were a well-to-do Muslim couple whose ancestors could be traced to the prophet Mohammad, the founder of Islam. Musharaff's father, Syed Musharaff-ud-Din, was a career

Pervez Musharraf and Donald H. Rumsfeld address a press conference. Pakistan pledged to fight terrorism after September 11.

diplomat able to maintain a gracious home in an elite neighborhood. Musharaff's mother, Zohra, worked at home caring for her three sons. She also served with the International Labor Organization, a United Nations agency that focuses on social justice and improving the rights and working conditions of laborers worldwide.

When he was four years old Musharraf and his family moved from Hindu-dominated India to Pakistan, a country that had once been part of India and had been created in 1947 as a Muslim state. Musharraf's father was soon assigned to Ankara, Turkey, however; from 1949 to 1956 Musharraf went to school there and learned to speak Turkish fluently. Because he was short and plump during those years, his classmates nicknamed him Gola (ball).

When it came time to attend high school, Musharraf's parents sent him back to Pakistan to the prestigious Saint Patrick's High School in Karachi. He later attended Forman Christian College, the alma mater of many notables in Pakistan, in Lahore. There he developed an interest in competitive athletics, and, with exercise, his baby fat turned to muscle.

In 1961, when he was eighteen, Musharraf joined the Pakistan Military Academy in Kakul in northwestern Pakistan. Although he was not at the top of his class, Musharraf earned honors for excelling in a combination of academics and physical training. "There wasn't a game he couldn't learn," remembers one of his classmates at the academy. Musharraf went on to be commissioned in the elite Artillery Regiment in 1964 and was remembered in the yearbook as "Quite a guy to be with, especially when in a fix."[122]

Military Career

As a young officer Musharraf saw action in Pakistan's 1965 war with India (the second Kashmir War) and was awarded the Imtiazi Sanad, a medal for bravery. He also saw action in the third Kashmir War in 1971, this time as commander of a squadron of commandos from the Special Service Group (comparable to the Green Berets). The group was known for its physical prowess and its willingness to confront danger. "I was always a risktaker,"[123] Musharraf later noted.

As his career progressed, Musharraf married on December 28, 1968. He and his wife Sehba had a daughter and a son. Musharraf was a devoted family man, and also found time to enjoy a variety of sports including badminton, golf, canoeing, and sailing.

Musharraf rose through the army ranks serving as commander of armored divisions, infantry brigades, and as director of general military operations at General Headquarters in Rawalpindi, near Islamabad. Through it all his men liked and respected Musharraf for his helpfulness, honesty, and fair-mindedness. "We found him everywhere the troops were. He was able to inspire them,"[124] says a friend. At about this time Musharraf also furthered was also appointed chairman of the Joint Chiefs of Staff.

In 1999, however, he faced a confrontation with Prime Minister Nawaz Sharif, Pakistan's corrupt leader. Sharif wanted to weaken the power of the military, which was the only force in the country strong enough to challenge his power. On October 12, 1999, while returning from a visit to Sri Lanka, Musharraf discovered that Sharif had fired him and was refusing to let his plane land at the Karachi airport. Sharif was highly unpopular with the army, however, and the troops rebelled against his orders. Staging a military coup the troops surrounded Sharif's home, held him prisoner, and allowed Musharraf to land. In sympathy with their stance, Musharraf decided that circumstances warranted a military takeover of the country. He suspended the constitution but hastened to reassure his people that conditions in the government were "calm, stable and under control."[125] Sharif was later sent into exile in Saudi Arabia.

As soon as possible Musharraf addressed the nation at greater length. He pointed out that Sharif's government, although democratically elected, had been systematically destroying the country. The prime minister had rewritten the constitution, ignored the judiciary, undermined the military, and driven the

Musharraf and his wife, Sehba, pose in front of the Taj Mahal. Born in India, Musharraf moved to Pakistan as a child.

his military education by studying at Britain's Royal College of Defense Studies in London while he wrote a thesis on the Indo-Pakistan arms race and its impact on socioeconomic development in those two countries.

Controversial Decision

As a result of his intelligence and leadership skills Musharraf was promoted to chief of army staff in 1998. On April 9, 1999, he

Desperate Measures

After taking over his country in a bloodless coup, General Pervez Musharraf spoke to his people in a speech entitled "Address to the Nation by Chief Executive Islamic Republic of Pakistan." The address, given on October 17, 1999, just five days after the coup, was published in *Dawn* newspaper and can be read in its entirety at Pakistani.org.

My dear countrymen! . . . Pakistan today stands at the crossroads of its destiny—a destiny which is in our hands to make or break. Fifty-two years ago, we started with a beacon of hope and today that beacon is no more and we stand in darkness. There is despondency, and hopelessness surrounding us with no light visible anywhere around. The slide down has been gradual but has rapidly accelerated in the last many years.

Today, we have reached a stage where our economy has crumbled, our credibility is lost, state institutions lie demolished; provincial disharmony has caused cracks in the federation, and people who were once brothers are now at each other's throat. . . .

Let us not be despondent. I am an optimist. I have faith in the destiny of this nation; belief in its people and conviction in its future. We were not a poor nation as generally perceived. In fact we are rich. We have fertile land that can produce three crops a year. We have abundant water to irrigate these lands and generate surplus power. We have gas, coal and vast untapped mineral resources— and above all a dynamic and industrious people. All these await mobilization. We have only to awaken, join hands and grasp our destiny. For Allah helps those who help themselves. . . .

Quite clearly, what Pakistan has experienced in the recent years has been hardly a label of democracy not the essence of it. Our people were never emancipated from the yoke of despotism. I shall not allow the people to be taken back to the era of sham democracy but to a true one. And I promise you I will Inshallah [God willing].

economy toward collapse through spending heavily, misusing taxes, and even laundering illegal money.

For his part Musharraf promised to work for a revival of the economy, tax reform, and better international relations. "This is not martial law, only another path towards democracy," he stated in a televised address. "The armed forces have no intention to stay in charge any longer than is absolutely necessary to pave the way for true democracy to flourish in Pakistan."[126]

Coups were not unusual occurrences in Pakistan; this was the fourth takeover in

five decades. The United States and other Western nations felt compelled to condemn the overthrow of a democratically elected government, however. They saw Musharraf as a potential dictator who was also a supporter of Pakistan's test detonation of an atomic bomb in 1998 and a backer of the Taliban government in Afghanistan. "People who do that [threaten and kill Americans] are our enemies, and people who support those people will also be treated as our enemies,"[127] a high-ranking U.S. official told Pakistan's intelligence chief, General Mahmoud Ahmed.

Musharraf understood the West's condemnation. But he was not as strong a supporter of the Taliban as he appeared. Although Pakistan extended full recognition to the repressive government (and was one of the few nations in the world to do so), Musharraf noted in April 2001, "[We recognized the Taliban for] national security, pure and simple. We have one big threat from the east with India. We have no desire to add another threat from the west with Afghanistan."[128]

A Key Partner

Pakistan remained loyal to the Taliban and out of favor with the United States until the days following the September 11, 2001, attacks on the World Trade Center and the Pentagon. The United States still condemned Musharraf's past actions, but by then it had observed that he did not behave like a repressive tyrant. Indeed, Musharraf seemed to be a proponent of a moderate, stable government, so the United States chose to ignore his past in order to pursue its present goals. As George W. Bush declared war on terrorism, U.S. officials made contact with Musharraf. They appealed to him to cooperate by sharing any information he had about al-Qaeda, cracking down on all al-Qaeda activities in his country, and complying with future requests the U.S. government might make.

In a move that gratified the United States, Musharraf agreed. On September 13, 2001, he issued a statement emphasizing his country's disapproval of terrorism and guaranteeing its full cooperation in the coming war. "Pakistan is committing all of its resources in an effort coordinated with the United States to locate and punish those involved in this horrific act,"[129] he stated.

His statement was the beginning of a new chapter in Pakistan history. On November 10, 2001, and again on February 13, 2002, Musharraf flew to the United States to meet with President Bush. Together the two leaders agreed to forge closer ties between their countries. In return for Musharraf's cooperation Bush announced that he would erase Pakistan's debt of $36 million, lift past economic and military sanctions against Pakistan, and grant the country more than a billion dollars in aid. Bush also pledged to work to strengthen investment and trade ties, and help promote development and educational opportunities for Pakistanis. "President Musharraf is a leader with courage and vision, and his nation is a key partner in the global coalition against terror,"[130] Bush said to the media in Washington on February 13.

Putting Words into Action

On his return to Pakistan Musharraf set out to do his part in the war against terrorism. He banned terrorist groups, closed their offices, and ordered the arrest of their members. He authorized new measures to curb the inflammatory teaching of militant Islam in the eight thousand *madrassas* throughout the country, and backed up his moves with tough penalties: Those who disobeyed would face prison terms of up to two years. "No madrassas will be allowed to indulge in militancy,"[131] Minister for Religious Affairs Mehmood Ghazi told reporters at a press conference.

Musharraf also directed thousands of Pakistan troops to hunt down and arrest suspected al-Qaeda and Taliban militants.

The Key to Musharraf

In an article entitled "Pervez, The Friendly Dictator," found online at the website of Carnegie Endowment for International Peace, journalist George Perkovich explains the Pakistani president's view of democracy and his conviction that he is vital to the future of his country.

"True democracy" has two elements, Musharraf explained. . . . "One is having an elected government. Two is how that government functions. . . . People say I am not elected, but the true essence of democracy is there now." How is that so? Well, because Musharraf feels he's a democrat. "Unless there is unity of command, unless there is one man in charge on top," he says, democracy will not function. To many this might seem like dictatorship, but Musharraf truly does not see it that way.

The key to understanding Pervez Musharraf is this: He is so sure of his own good will and altruism [unselfishness] that he fails to see how others could doubt him. "I know it sounds arrogant," he told me. "It sounds arrogant to me when I say it. But I think I am the only person who can make sure that true democracy takes root and is allowed to function without being pulled down."

At the same time he gave U.S. troops permission to use Pakistan's air bases, share its intelligence, and, in some cases, follow fugitive Taliban and al-Qaeda forces from Afghanistan into Pakistan.

In June 2002, Pakistan troops moved into remote mountainous regions in western Pakistan, an area that was ordinarily under tribal rule. There they established border checkpoints and engaged in air and ground operations to flush out al-Qaeda suspects who were believed to be hiding in mountain caves.

Troops also conducted house-to-house searches in settlements in the region. In one clash in June 2002, about fifty Pakistani soldiers struck an al-Qaeda compound located in Azam Warsak, about twenty miles from the Afghan border. Because the area was residential, tanks and planes could not be used, so troops stormed the gates of the compound. They were hit by machine-gun fire and grenades. After a two-hour battle ten Pakistanis and two al-Qaeda fighters lay dead. "[Patrolling the tribal regions] is a difficult task," stated CNN reporter Kamal Hyder, who visited the area in question. "The [Pakistani] army admits that it is a difficult task, and there are strains on the army's budgets when they're on a war footing. But the morale here is very high and most people we spoke to told us that it was Pakistan's duty to the international community to show that Pakistan was with the international community and its war against terror."[132]

Musharraf and Rumsfeld arrive at the Pentagon in February 2002. Musharraf is trying to purge Pakistan of militant Islamic groups like al-Qaeda and the Taliban.

Breaking the Terrorist Network

Over the course of a year Pakistan forces captured dozens of suspected militants. Several were fugitives of some renown. In February 2002 militants Ahmed Omar Saeed Sheikh, Salman Saqib, Fahad Naseem, and Shaikh Adil—who were responsible for the January 2002 abduction and murder of the *Wall Street Journal* reporter Daniel Pearl in Karachi—were arrested. Pearl's death deeply embarrassed Musharraf because it exposed his inability to control crime and keep militant Islamic groups in check.

Tried and found guilty in Pakistan, Ahmed Sheikh was sentenced to death. The other three men received life sentences.

White House spokesman Ari Fleischer noted, "Daniel Pearl was brutally executed, and Pakistan's court system has now ruled. This is a further example of Pakistan showing leadership in the war against terror."[133]

The terrorist network was also damaged when Abu Zubaydah, the man allegedly in charge of terrorist training camps in Afghanistan, was seized in Pakistan in April 2002. Zubaydah was a senior member of the al-Qaeda network and was also allegedly responsible for planning new

Ahmed Omar Saeed Sheikh, one of the men who abducted and murdered journalist Daniel Pearl, was arrested in Pakistan and sentenced to death.

attacks on U.S. interests. In early September 2002, Pakistan police arrested Ramzi Binalshibh, another high-profile fugitive. Binalshibh, a Yemini national, was the suspected organizer of the September 11 attacks and was a key conveyor of money and information between bin Laden in Afghanistan and the hijack teams in the United States. Binalshibh was captured in Karachi, along with eleven other al-Qaeda suspects. "The recent action taken by the law enforcement agencies against terrorist networks, especially al-Qaeda, has improved the law and order situation in Pakistan," Musharraf said. "The police, the (paramilitary) Rangers and the intelligence agencies have broken the terrorist network."[134]

Musharraf had become a hero to the West for his commitment to eradicating terrorism in Pakistan. He also appeared to be trying to improve relations with neighboring India, a longtime adversary. In July 2001, he visited that country, emphasizing that he wanted to do his part to settle old differences. "I have come here to end the politics of hatred," he told Indian academics at a reception held at the Pakistani mission in Delhi. "When it comes to peace efforts you will not find me wanting."[135] (Hostilities with India over the disputed region of Kashmir flared up again in 2002, and again Musharraf emphasized that his country did not want war with its neighbor.)

Betrayer of Islam?

Despite his improved standing with the rest of the world, within his own country

Musharraf faced bitter criticism and growing opposition from parts of the population who considered his pro-American stance a betrayal of Islam. In October 2001, over ten thousand radical students and members of Islamic groups expressed their disapproval by rioting in the streets of Quetta, burning buildings, smashing cars, and chanting "Down with America." In Peshawar eight hundred militant students fought for two hours with riot police. In Karachi several hundred people set buses on fire and threw rocks at police. "We are ready to fight," said twenty-year-old Zahoor Mehdi. "I have told my parents that I will go to Afghanistan, and they have granted me permission."[136]

Musharraf was quick to point out that even though thousands of Pakistanis had taken to the streets in protest, they were a small minority of the country's 140 million people. He continued to maintain that most Pakistanis wanted their country to become prosperous, democratic, and moderate. One ordinary citizen who supported this view testified,

> I believe the General is doing a great job, he has put the country back on the track of becoming a developed country. The actions he has taken will have a positive long term effect on Pakistan and its people. He has also showed that Pakistan is not afraid of any external dangers. He is far better than those corrupt politicians who have ruled and ruined the country for the past 53 years.[137]

As time passed large public protests waned, but opposition remained strong. In June 2002 a car bomb exploded outside the U.S. consulate in Karachi. It was the fourth attack against foreigners in Pakistan since January. In July 2002 educators who resented the president's law regulating *madrassas* threatened to demonstrate if the changes were not revoked.

Parliamentary elections in October 2002 were the strongest evidence of

Vulnerable to Criticism

In an article entitled "America's New Alliance with Pakistan: Avoiding the Traps of the Past," published online by the Carnegie Endowment for International Peace, Husain Haqqani (a visiting scholar for the organization) points out the shortcomings of military regimes and their unpopularity with the people of Pakistan.

No matter how initially promising they have seemed, military dictators have always ended up multiplying Pakistan's problems instead of solving them. Repression at home and confrontation with India have characterized each of Pakistan's past military regimes. The focus on austerity dictated by heavy military spending . . . has inflicted economic hardship on the poor. The U.S. association with these military regimes has led to diminished popular sentiment in support of the United States.

General Musharraf's regime seems firmly in control for now, and he has so far managed to contain his critics. But the unrepresentative character of his government leaves it vulnerable to criticism in a country that has yearned for democracy since independence.

Musharraf's unpopularity. An alliance of the country's radical Islamic parties, known as Muttahida Majlis-e-Amal (MMA), secured 48 out of 272 seats in Parliament, a significant increase of its power. Religious parties had only won two seats in Parliament in the 1997 elections. "It is a revolution," MMA vice president Qazi Hussain Ahmed stated. "People wanted a change from the past corrupt rulers and Musharraf's pro-U.S. policies. The widespread anti-American feeling among the people has clearly gone in our favour and we are very happy about it."[138]

Musharraf, who retained his presidency, made the best of the situation. He expressed satisfaction with the democratic process. And he hoped that all political parties and successful candidates would strive for the establishment of a stable, honest, forward-looking government that would work for progress and the development of Pakistan.

"Progress but Not Westernization"

There is no doubt that Musharraf faces difficult times ahead if he continues as president of Pakistan working to rebuild his country, to become a member of the world community, and at the same time to satisfy those who do not welcome close ties to the West. "We want progress but not Westernization. We can be both progressive and religious at the same time,"[139] he points out.

Despite enemies who believe he is a traitor and skeptics who insist he is a self-serving dictator, Musharraf's reputation as an honest man, a clear thinker, and a man of principle continues to grow. Only time and events will reveal how he will go down in history, however. As one journalist noted after meeting him, "He [may be] what many associates say he is: a straight man who is trying to do what he thinks is best for his country."[140]

☆ Notes ☆

Introduction: Combatants in the War on Terrorism

1. Quoted in *PBS Frontline*, "Who Is Osama Bin Laden?" May 1998. www.jihadunspun.net.
2. *Aljazeera*, "Transcript of Bin Laden's October 2001 Interview," October 2001. www.jihadunspun.net.
3. George W. Bush, "President Bush Speaks to the United Nations," *The White House*, November 10, 2001. www.whitehouse.gov.
4. George W. Bush, "President Delivers the State of the Union Address," *The White House*, January 29, 2002. www.whitehouse.gov.

Chapter 1: Osama bin Laden: Most Wanted Fugitive

5. Quoted in *Cable News Network*, "Bush: Bin Laden 'Prime Suspect,'" September 17, 2001. www.cnn.com.
6. Quoted in Jason Burke, "The Making of Osama Bin Laden," *Observer*, October 28, 2001. www.observer.co.uk.
7. Quoted in Joyce Rappaport, "Weekly Quotes," *Canadian Institute for Jewish Research*, 2002. www.isranet.org.
8. Quoted in Burke, "The Making of Osama Bin Laden."

9. Quoted in *PBS Frontline*, "A Biography of Osama Bin Laden," 2001. www.pbs.org.
10. Quoted in Burke, "The Making of Osama Bin Laden."
11. Quoted in Burke, "The Making of Osama Bin Laden."
12. Quoted in Burke, "The Making of Osama Bin Laden."
13. Quoted in Robert Fisk, "Anti-Soviet Warrior Puts His Army on the Road to Peace," *Independent*, 1993. www.jihadunspun.net.
14. Quoted in Burke, The Making of Osama Bin Laden."
15. Quoted in Peter Bergen and Frank Smyth, "Holy Warrior Redux," *New Republic Online*, September 14, 2001. www.thenewrepublic.com.
16. Quoted in Rahimullah Yousafsai, "ABC Interview with Osama Bin Laden," *Jihad Unspun*, January 1998. www.jihadunspun.net.
17. John J. Lumpkin, "A Bin Laden Son, 22, Is Rising Star in al-Qaida," *Seattle Times*, July 30, 2002. seattletimes.nwsource.com.
18. Quoted in *Cable News Network*, "U.S. Official Sees Similarities Between

USS Cole Blast and Embassy Attacks," October 23, 2000. www.cnn.com.

19. Quoted in *Cable News Network*, "Bin Laden Praises USS Cole Bombers," March 1, 2001. www.cnn.com.

20. Quoted in Yousafsai, "ABC Interview with Osama Bin Laden."

21. George W. Bush, "Presidential Speech at the Pentagon," *The Patriot Resource*, September 17, 2001. www.patriotresource.com.

22. Quoted in Yousafsai, "ABC Interview with Osama Bin Laden."

23. Quoted in *MSNBC*, "Osama Bin Laden: FAQ," 2002. www.msnbc.com.

24. Quoted in Yousafsai, "ABC Interview with Osama Bin Laden."

Chapter 2: George W. Bush: Commander in Chief

25. Quoted in *Online News Hour*, "You Have Made a GREAT Choice," July 21, 2000. www.pbs.org.

26. George W. Bush, *A Charge to Keep*. New York: Morrow, 1999, p. 15.

27. Quoted in *Washington Post*, "The Life of George W. Bush," 1999. www.washingtonpost.com.

28. Quoted in Bill Minutaglio, *First Son: George W. Bush and the Bush Family Dynasty*. New York: Times Books, 1999, p. 49.

29. Bush, *A Charge to Keep*, p. 21.

30. Quoted in Minutaglio, *First Son*, p. 62.

31. Bush, *A Charge to Keep*, p. 54.

32. Bush, *A Charge to Keep*, p. 3.

33. Bush, *A Charge to Keep*, p. 185.

34. Bush, *A Charge to Keep*, p. 224.

35. George W. Bush, "President George W. Bush's Inaugural Address," *The White House*, January 20, 2001. www.whitehouse.gov.

36. George W. Bush "Statement by the President in His Address to the Nation," *The White House*, September 11, 2001. www.whitehouse.gov.

37. George W. Bush, "Address to a Joint Session of Congress and the American People," *The White House*, September 20, 2001. www.whitehouse.gov.

38. Quoted in J. Michael Waller, "Command Performance," *Insight on the News*, March 4, 2002, p. 12.

39. George W. Bush, "Radio Address of the President to the Nation," *The White House*, October 6, 2001. www.whitehouse.gov.

40. Quoted in *ComputerUser.com*, "National Fatherhood Initiative," December 22, 2002. www.computeruser.com.

41. Bush, "Address to a Joint Session of Congress and the American People."

42. Quoted in *Cable News Network*, "Bush Offers Condolences to the Afghan People," July 2, 2002. www.cnn.com.

43. Bush, "Address to a Joint Session of Congress and the American People."

Chapter 3: Tommy Franks: The "Soldier's General"

44. Quoted in *Cable News Network*, "Gen. Tom Franks: A Silent Partner in Operation Enduring Freedom," October 24, 2001. www.cnn.com.

45. Quoted in Cal Fussman, "What I've Learned," *Esquire*, August 2002. www.esquire.com.

46. Quoted in George Edmonson, "Gen. Tommy Franks Makes a Deeper Impression Now than in the Past," *Cox Newspapers*, February 3, 2002. www.coxnews.com.

47. Quoted in Paul De La Garza, "A Man and His Mission," *St. Petersburg Times*, December 12, 2001. www.spti mes.com.

48. Quoted in Mark Permenter, "Commanding Presence," *Uta Magazine Online*, Fall 2002. www.utamagazine. uta.edu.

49. Quoted in Permenter, "Commanding Presence."

50. Quoted in Fussman, "What I've Learned."

51. Quoted in Thomas Field-Meyer and Don Sider, "Man with a Mission," *People Weekly*, October 29, 2001, p. 81.

52. Quoted in Field-Meyer and Sider, "Man with a Mission," p. 81.

53. Quoted in Barbara Starr, "As Pentagon Burned, Plans for War Took Shape," *Cable News Network*, September 6, 2002. www.cnn.com.

54. Quoted in Field-Meyer and Sider, "Man with a Mission," p. 81.

55. Quoted in De La Garza, "A Man and His Mission."

56. Quoted in Kathleen T. Rhem, "Franks: A Leader Sure of His Mission and His Troops," *American Forces Information Service News Articles*, January 5, 2002. www.defenselink. mil.

57. Quoted in Matt Ward, "Alumnus Leads U.S. Military Effort," *Shorthorn Online*, October 10, 2001. www.theshorthorn.com.

58. Quoted in Linda D. Kozaryn, "Ask the Boss, He'll Tell It Like It Is," *American Forces Information Services News Articles*, February 1, 2001. www.defenselink.mil.

59. Quoted in Jeannette Steele, "Army General Tries His Sea Legs," *San Diego Union-Tribune*, December 26, 2001. www.signonsandiego.com.

60. Quoted in Edmonson, "Gen. Tommy Franks Makes a Deeper Impression."

61. Quoted in David Wastell, "General's Caution Dismays Rumsfeld," *Telegraph*, November 15, 2002. www.telegraph.co.uk.

62. Quoted in Duncan Campbell, "Tommy Franks: He's No Stormin' Norman," *Guardian*, November 17, 2001. www.guardian.co.uk.

63. Tommy R. Franks and Mark Thompson, "Our People Were Shot At, *Time*, March 4, 2002, p. 35.

64. Quoted in Rhem, "Franks: A Leader Sure of His Mission and His Troops."

65. Quoted in De La Garza, "A Man and His Mission."

Chapter 4: Mohammad Omar: Commander of the Faithful

66. Barry Bearak, "Once Vigilantes, Now Strict Rulers," *New York Times*, September 19, 2001, p. B6.

67. Quoted in Rashmee Z. Ahmed, "Mullah Omar Mentally Unstable, Says Doctor," *Times of India*, October 7, 2001. http://timesofindia.indiatimes.com.

68. Michael Griffin, *Reaping the Whirlwind: The Taliban Movement in Afghanistan*. London: Pluto Press, 2001, p. 33.

69. Quoted in Griffin, *Reaping the Whirlwind*, p. 35.

70. Quoted in Griffin, *Reaping the Whirlwind*, p. 3.

71. Quoted in Robert Marquand, "The Reclusive Ruler Who Runs the Taliban," *Christian Science Monitor*, October 10, 2001. www. csmonitor.com.

72. Quoted in Jonathan Harley, "Taliban Moves to Encourage Af-ghani Refugees to Return," *World Today*, November 23, 1999. www.abc.net.au.

73. Griffin, *Reaping the Whirlwind*, p. 60.

74. Quoted in Penney Kome, "Lifting the Shroud," *Disability World*, March 2000. www.disabilityworld.org.

75. Quoted in Rory McCarthy, "Taliban Order All Statues Destroyed," *Guardian Unlimited*, February 27, 2001. www.guardian.co.uk.

76. Quoted in Marquand, "The Reclusive Ruler."

77. Quoted in Joshua Hammer and John Barry, "A Win in the Fog of War," *Newsweek*, November 19, 2001, p. 24.

78. Quoted in *Office of International Information Programs, U.S. Department of State*, "The End of the Reign of Terror in Afghanistan," December 12, 2001. www.globalsecurity.org.

79. Richard Armitage, "Modification of Description of 'Territory of Afghanistan Controlled by the Taliban,'" *Federal Register*, January 29, 2002. www.bxa.doc.gov.

80. *Guardian Unlimited*, "Mullah Omar—In His Own Words," September 26, 2001. www.guardian.co.uk.

Chapter 5: Hamid Karzai: Leader of a Broken Nation

81. Ed Warner, "Karzai's Prospects," *Global Security*, December 18, 2002. www.globalsecurity.org.

82. Quoted in Kathy Gannon, "Afghan Girls Head Back to School," *North County Times*, March 24, 2002. www.nctimes.net.

83. Quoted in *Cable News Network*, "Hamid Karzai, No Stranger to Leadership," September 5, 2002. www.cnn.com.

84. Quoted in Donald Angus, "New Leader Has All the Credentials," *South China Morning Post*, December 6, 2001. http://special.scmp.com.

85. *BBC News*, "Hamid Karzai: Talking Point Special," May 10, 2002. http://news.bbc.co.uk.

86. Quoted in Pam O'Toole, "Hamid Karzai," *Watan Afghanistan*, 2002. www.afghanan.net.

87. Quoted in Angus, "New Leader."
88. Quoted in Angus, "New Leader."
89. Quoted in Paul Michael Christie, "Afghan Anti-Taliban Leader Appeals for Foreign Aid," *Afghan Info Center*, November 8, 2002. www. afghaninfo.com.
90. *PBS Frontline*, "Interview: U.S. Army Captain Jason Amerine," July 9–12, 2002. www.pbs.org.
91. *PBS Frontline*, "Interview: President Hamid Karzai," May 7, 2002. www.pbs.org.
92. Quoted in Angus, "New Leader."
93. Quoted in *Afghanland*, "Who Is Hamid Karzai?" 2000. www.afghanland. com.
94. Quoted in *Time International*, "New Style of Government," March 4, 2002, p. 12.
95. Quoted in Patricia Smith, "Karzai's Quest: The Man and the Plan," *New York Times Upfront*, February 11, 2002, p. 22.
96. Quoted in *Cable News Network*, "Karzai Pleads with Afghan Expatriates to Return," January 28, 2002. www.cnn.com.
97. Quoted in Charles Recknagel and Azam Gorgin, "Afghanistan: Karzai Speaks of Accomplishments, Problems in First Months," *Radio Free Europe*, April 10, 2002. www.rferl.org.
98. Quoted in Jan Goodwin, "An Uneasy Peace: Afghan Women Are Free of the Taliban, but Liberation Is Still a Distant Dream," *Nation*, April 29, 2002, p. 20.
99. Quoted in Humayun Akhtar, "Karzai—A Hero in the Making?" *Pakistan Link*, December 14, 2001. www. pakistanlink.com.
100. Quoted in *Cable News Network*, "Taliban Blamed in Karzai Attack," September 8, 2002. http:// asia.cnn.com.
101. Quoted in *United Press International*, "US Worries About Karzai's Isolation," August 25, 2002, p. 4.
102. Quoted in *Cable News Network*, "Hamid Karzai, No Stranger to Leadership."

Chapter 6: Abdul Rashid Dostum: Seasoned Warrior

103. Robert Young Pelton, "The Legend of Heavy D & the Boys," *National Geographic Adventure*, March 2002, p. 66.
104. Quoted in Camelia Entekhabi-Fard, "More Important than a Position in the Government Is Keeping the Peace," *EurasiaNet*, April 24, 2002. www.eurasianet.org.
105. Quoted in Patrick Cockburn, "Rashid Dostum: The Treacherous General," *Independent*, (U.K.) December 1, 2001. www.zmag.org.
106. Quoted in John F. Burns, "Afghan Fights Islamic Tide; As a Savior or a Conqueror," *New York Times*, October 14, 1997. www.pulitzer.org.
107. Quoted in Burns, "Afghan Fights Islamic Tide."
108. Quoted in Pelton, "The Legend of Heavy D & the Boys," p. 66.

109. Quoted in Burns, "Afghan Fights Islamic Tide."

110. Quoted in Pelton, "The Legend of Heavy D & the Boys," p. 66.

111. Quoted in Pelton, "The Legend of Heavy D & the Boys," p. 67.

112. Quoted in Pelton, "The Legend of Heavy D & the Boys," p. 67.

113. Quoted in Pelton, "The Legend of Heavy D & the Boys," p. 66.

114. Quoted in Robert Young Pelton, "Afghan War Eyewitness on Warlords, Future, More," *National Geographic News*, February 15, 2002. http://news.nationalgeographic.com.

115. Quoted in Hammer and Barry, "A Win in the Fog of War," p. 24.

116. Quoted in Pelton, "The Legend of Heavy D & the Boys," p. 70.

117. Quoted in Pamela Constable, "Operation Transformation for Afghan with a Dark Past," *Washington Post*, May 29, 2002. www.washingtonpost.com.

118. Quoted in Richard S. Ehrlich, "Dostum: America's Gruesome New Ally?" *Laissez Faire City Times*, December 31, 2001. www.geocities.com.

119. Quoted in Shyam Bhatia, "Karzai Entrusts Defense Portfolio to Pro-India Fahim," *Rediff.com*, June 20, 2002. www.rediff.com.

120. Quoted in Camelia Entekhabi-Fard, "Violence Thwarts Northern Afghan City's Rehabilitation," *EurasiaNet*, July 1, 2002. www.eurasianet.org.

121. Quoted in Ehrlich, "Dostum: America's Gruesome New Ally?"

Chapter 7: Pervez Musharraf: Pakistan's Risk Taker

122. Quoted in Anthony Spaeth, "Dangerous Ground," *Time Asia*, July 22, 2002. www.time.com.

123. Quoted in Spaeth, "Dangerous Ground."

124. Quoted in Spaeth, "Dangerous Ground."

125. Quoted in *Cable News Network*, "Army Chief: Pakistan Coup Launched 'as Last Resort,'" October 13, 1999. www.cnn.com.

126. *Islamic Republic of Pakistan*, "Chief Executive's Interview with the *Washington Times*," March 21, 2001. www.pak.gov.pk.

127. Quoted in Barton Gellman, "Clinton's War on Terror," *Washington Post*, December 19, 2001. www.washingtonpost.com.

128. Quoted in Arnaud De Borchgrave, "Pakistan's Leader Vows to Establish Democracy," *Insight on the News*, April 30, 2001, p. 30.

129. Quoted in *Cable News Network*, "Bush Administration Puts Pressure on Pakistan," September 13, 2001. www.cnn.com.

130. Quoted in *U.S. Department of State*, "Bush Hosts Pakistani President Musharraf at White House," February 13, 2002. http://usinfo.state.gov.

131. Quoted in Jack Kelley, "Pakistan to

Ban Teaching Radical Islam," *USA Today*, June 21, 2002. www.usato day.com.

132. *Cable News Network*, "Kamal Hyder: Pakistan Searches for al-Qaeda Fighters," December 21, 2001. www.cnn.com.

133. Quoted in *BBC News*, "Death Sought for Pearl Killers," July 16, 2002. http://news.bbc.co.uk.

134. Quoted in *CourtTV*, "Police Link Pearl Killer to al-Qaida," September 17, 2002. www.courttv.com.

135. Quoted in *BBC News*, "Musharraf Seeks Fresh Start with India," July 14, 2001. http://news.bbc.co.uk.

136. Quoted in Michael A. Lev, "Pakistan Quells Anti-US Protests," *Chicago Tribune*, October 9, 2001. www.chicagotribune.com.

137. Quoted in *BBC News*, "Has Musharraf Been Good News for Pakistan?" October 12, 2000. http://news.bbc.co.uk.

138. Quoted in Muhammad Najeeb, "Pakistan Heads for Hung Parliament," *Indo-Asian News Service*, October 11, 2002. http://in.news.yahoo.com.

139. Quoted in *Christian Century*, "Quote, Unquote," January 30, 2002, p. 16.

140. Jason Burke, "Musharraf Shows Off His Happy Family and the Two Little 'Doggies,'" *Express India.com*, October 20, 1999. www.expressin dia.com.

★ For Further Reading ★

D.J. Herda, *The Afghan Rebels: The War in Afghanistan*. New York: Franklin Watts, 1990. History of tribal and religious issues in the 1980 Soviet-Afghan War.

Latifa and Chekeba Hachemi, *My Forbidden Face: Growing Up Under the Taliban*. New York: Hyperion, 2001. Account of the life of a young Afghan girl growing up under Taliban rule.

Elaine Landau, *Osama bin Laden: A War Against the West*. Brookfield, CT: Twenty-First Century Books, 2002. Biography of the radical terrorist leader.

Peter Marsden, *The Taliban: War, Religion and the New Order in Afghanistan*. Karachi, Pakistan: Oxford University Press, 1998. Explores the Taliban's philosophy, its rise to power, and its war with the Northern Alliance.

☆ Works Consulted ☆

Books

George W. Bush, *A Charge to Keep.* New York: Morrow, 1999. First-person account of Bush's life prior to becoming president.

Michael Griffin, *Reaping the Whirlwind: The Taliban Movement in Afghanistan.* London: Pluto Press, 2001. Eyewitness account of conflict in Afghanistan prior to the United States's arrival. Explores the Taliban's connections with Osama bin Laden.

Bill Minutaglio, *First Son: George W. Bush and the Bush Family Dynasty.* New York: Times Books, 1999. Biography of George W. Bush prior to his presidency.

Periodicals

Barry Bearak, "Once Vigilantes, Now Strict Rulers," *New York Times*, September 19, 2001.

Christian Century, "Quote, Unquote," January 30, 2002.

Arnaud De Borchgrave, "Pakistan's Leader Vows to Establish Democracy," *Insight on the News*, April 30, 2001.

Thomas Field-Meyer and Don Sider, "Man with a Mission," *People Weekly*, October 29, 2001.

Tommy R. Franks and Mark Thompson, "Our People Were Shot At," *Time*, March 4, 2002.

Jan Goodwin, "An Uneasy Peace: Afghan Women Are Free of the Taliban, but Liberation Is Still a Distant Dream," *Nation*, April 29, 2002.

Joshua Hammer and John Barry, "A Win in the Fog of War," *Newsweek*, November 19, 2001.

Robert Young Pelton, "The Legend of Heavy D & the Boys," *National Geographic Adventure*, March 2002.

Patricia Smith, "Karzai's Quest: The Man and the Plan," *New York Times Upfront*, February 11, 2002.

Time International, "New Style of Government," March 4, 2002.

United Press International, "US Worries About Karzai's Isolation," August 25, 2002.

J. Michael Waller, "Command Performance," *Insight on the News*, March 4, 2002.

Internet Sources

Afghanland, "Who Is Hamid Karzai?" 2000. www.afghanland.com.

Rashmee Z. Ahmed, "Mullah Omar Mentally Unstable, Says Doctor," *Times of*

India, October 7, 2001. http://time sofindia.indiatimes.com.

Humayun, Akhtar, "Karzai—A Hero in the Making?" *Pakistan Link,* December 14, 2001. www.pakistanlink.com.

Aljazeera, "Transcript of Bin Laden's October 2001 Interview," October 2001. www.jihadunspun.net.

Donald Angus, "New Leader Has All the Credentials," *South China Morning Post,* December 6, 2001. http://special. scmp.com.

Richard Armitage, "Modification of Description of 'Territory of Afghanistan Controlled by the Taliban,'" *Federal Register,* January 29, 2002. www.bxa. doc.gov.

BBC News, "Death Sought for Pearl Killers," July 16, 2002. http://news.bbc.co.uk.

———, "Hamid Karzai: Talking Point Special," May 10, 2002. http://news.bbc. co.uk.

———, "Has Musharraf Been Good News for Pakistan?" October 12, 2000. http://news.bbc.co.uk.

———, "Musharraf Seeks Fresh Start with India," July 14, 2001. http:// news.bbc.co.uk.

———, "What is a Loya Jirga?" July 1, 2002. http://news.bbc.co.uk.

Peter Bergen and Frank Smyth, "Holy Warrior Redux," *New Republic Online,* September 14, 2001. www.thenewre public.com.

Shyam Bhatia, "Karzai Entrusts Defense Portfolio to Pro-India Fahim," *Rediff.com,* June 20, 2002. www.rediff.com.

Osama bin Laden, "Jihad Against Jews and Crusaders," *Jihad Unspun,* February 23, 1998. www.jihadunspun.net.

Jason Burke, "The Making of Osama Bin Laden," *Observer,* October 28, 2001. www.observer.co.uk.

———, "Musharraf Shows Off His Happy Family and the Two Little 'Doggies,'" *Express India.com,* October 20, 1999. www.expressindia.com.

John F. Burns, "Afghan Fights Islamic Tide; As a Savior or a Conqueror," *New York Times,* October 14, 1997. www.pulitzer.org.

George W. Bush, "Address to a Joint Session of Congress and the American People," *The White House,* September 20, 2001. www.whitehouse.gov.

———, "President Bush Speaks to the United Nations," *The White House,* November 10, 2001. www.whitehouse. gov.

———, "President Delivers the State of the Union Address," *The White House,* January 29, 2002. www.white house.gov.

———, "President George W. Bush's Inaugural Address," *The White House,* January 20, 2001. www.whitehouse.gov.

———, "Presidential Speech at the Pentagon," *The Patriot Resource,* September 17, 2001. www.patriotresource.com.

———, "Radio Address of the President to the Nation," *The White House,* October 6, 2001. www.whitehouse.gov.

———, "Statement by the President in His Address to the Nation," *The White*

House, September 11, 2001. www.white house.gov.

Sally Buzbee, "Digging Out bin Laden," *Arizona Daily Star,* November 21, 2001. www.azstar.net.com.

Cable News Network, "Army Chief: Pakistan Coup Launched 'as Last Resort,'" October 13, 1999. www.cnn.com.

———, "Bin Laden Praises USS Cole Bombers," March 1, 2001. www.cnn.com.

———, "Bush Administration Puts Pressure on Pakistan," September 13, 2001. www.cnn.com.

———, "Bush: Bin Laden 'Prime Suspect,'" September 17, 2001. www.cnn.com.

———, "Bush Offers Condolences to the Afghan People," July 2, 2002. www.cnn.com.

———, "Gen. Tom Franks: A Silent Partner in Operation Enduring Freedom," October 24, 2001. www.cnn.com.

———, "Hamid Karzai, No Stranger to Leadership," September 5, 2002. www.cnn.com.

———, "Kamal Hyder: Pakistan Searches for al-Qaeda Fighters," December 21, 2001. www.cnn.com.

———, "Karzai Pleads with Afghan Expatriates to Return," January 28, 2002. www.cnn.com.

———, "Taliban Blamed in Karzai Attack," September 8, 2002. http://asia.cnn.com.

———, "U.S. Official Sees Similarities Between USS Cole Blast and Embassy Attacks," October 23, 2000. www.cnn.com.

Duncan Campbell, "Tommy Franks: He's No Stormin' Norman," *Guardian,* November 17, 2001. www.guardian.co.uk.

Paul Michael Christie, "Afghan Anti-Taliban Leader Appeals for Foreign Aid," *Afghan Info Center,* November 8, 2002. www.afghan-info.com.

Patrick Cockburn, "Rashid Dostum: The Treacherous General," *Independent* (U.K.), December 1, 2001. www.zmag.org.

ComputerUser.com, "National Fatherhood Initiative," December 22, 2002. www.computeruser.com.

Pamela Constable "Operation Transformation for Afghan with a Dark Past," *Washington Post,* May 29, 2002. www.washingtonpost.com.

CourtTV, "Police Link Pearl Killer to al-Qaida," September 17, 2002. www.courttv.com.

Anthony Davis, "Makeover for a Warlord," *Time,* June 3, 2002. www.time.com.

Paul De La Garza, "A Man and His Mission," *St. Petersburg Times,* December 12, 2001. www.sptimes.com.

George Edmonson, "Gen. Tommy Franks Makes a Deeper Impression Now than in the Past," *Cox Newspapers,* February 3, 2002. www.coxnews.com.

Richard S. Ehrlich, "Dostum: America's Gruesome New Ally?" *Laissez Faire City Times,* December 31, 2001. www.geocities.com

Camelia Entekhabi-Fard, "More Important than a Position in the Government

Is Keeping the Peace," *EurasiaNet*, April 24, 2002. www.eurasianet.org.

———, "Violence Thwarts Northern Afghan City's Rehabilitation," *EurasiaNet*, July 1, 2002. www.eurasianet.org.

Robert Fisk, "Anti-Soviet Warrior Puts His Army on the Road to Peace," *Independent*, 1993. www.jihadunspun. net.

Cal Fussman, "What I've Learned," *Esquire*, August 2002. www.esquire.com.

Kathy Gannon, "Afghan Girls Head Back to School," *North County Times*, March 24, 2002. www.nctimes.net.

Barton Gellman, "Clinton's War on Terror," *Washington Post*, December 19, 2001. www.washingtonpost.com.

Guardian Unlimited, "Mullah Omar—In His Own Words," September 26, 2001. www.guardian.co.uk.

Hussein Haggani, "America's New Alliance with Pakistan: Avoiding Traps of the Past," *Carnegie Endowment for International Peace*, October 12, 2002. www.ceip.org.

Jonathan Harley, "Taliban Moves to Encourage Afghani Refugees to Return," *World Today*, November 23, 1999. www.abc.net.au.

John Hendren, "Afghanistan Yields Lessons for Pentagon's Next Targets," *Los Angeles Times*, January 21, 2002. www.globalsecurity.org.

Pamela Hess, "Karzai Elected Afghan Head of State," *Washington Times*, June 13, 2002. www.washtimes.com.

Human Rights Watch, "Afghanistan: The Massacre in Mazar-i-Sharif," November 1998. www.hrw.org.

Islamic Republic of Pakistan, "Chief Executive's Interview with the *Washington Times*," March 21, 2001. www.pak. gov.pk.

Jack Kelley, "Pakistan to Ban Teaching Radical Islam," *USA Today*, June 21, 2002. www.usatoday.com.

Laura King, "Who Are the Afghans? A Look at Ethnic Groups," *Arizona Daily Star*, November 13, 2001. www.azstar net.com.

Penney Kome, "Lifting the Shroud," *Disability World*, March 2000. www.disabili tyworld.org.

Linda D. Kozaryn, "Ask the Boss, He'll Tell It Like It Is," *American Forces Information Services News Articles*, February 1, 2001. www.defenselink.mil.

Michael A. Lev, "Pakistan Quells Anti-US Protests," *Chicago Tribune*, October 9, 2001. www.chicagotribune.com.

John J. Lumpkin, "A Bin Laden Son, 22, Is Rising Star in al-Qaida," *Seattle Times*, July 30, 2002. http://seattle times.nwsource.com.

Robert Marquand, "The Reclusive Ruler Who Runs the Taliban," *Christian Science Monitor*, October 10, 2001. www.csmonitor.com.

Rory McCarthy, "Taliban Order All Statues Destroyed," *Guardian Unlimited*, February 27, 2001. www.guardian. co.uk.

MSNBC, "Osama Bin Laden: FAQ," 2002. www.msnbc.com.

Richard B. Meyers, "Posture Statement of General Richard B. Myers, USAF, Chairman of the Joint Chiefs of Staff Before the 107th Congress Senate Appropriations Committee Subcommittee on Defense," *Department of Defense*, May 21, 2002. www.defenselink.mil.

Pervez Musharraf, "General Pervez Musharraf's Address to the Nation October 17, 1999," *Dawn*, October 18, 1999. www.pakistani.org.

Muhammad Najeeb, "Pakistan Heads for Hung Parliament," *Indo-Asian News Service*, October 11, 2002. http://in.news.yahoo.com

Office of International Information Programs, U.S. Department of State, "The End of the Reign of Terror in Afghanistan," December 12, 2001. www.globalsecurity.org.

Muhammad Omar, "Speech by Taliban Leader Mullah Muhammad Omar," *Boston Herald.com*, September 19, 2001. www.bostonherald.com.

Online News Hour, "You have Made a GREAT Choice," July 21, 2000. www.pbs.org.

Pam O'Toole, "Hamid Karzai," *Watan Afghanistan*, 2002. www.afghanan.net.

PBS Frontline, "A Biography of Osama Bin Laden," 2001. www.pbs.org.

———, "Interview: President Hamid Karzai," May 7, 2002. www.pbs.org.

———, "Interview: U.S. Army Captain Jason Amerine," July 9–12, 2002. www.pbs.org.

———, "Who Is Osama bin Laden?" May, 1998. www.jihadunspun.net.

Robert Young Pelton, "Afghan War Eyewitness on Warlords, Future, More," *National Geographic News*, February 15, 2002. http://news.nationalgeographic.com.

George Perkovich, "Pervez, The Friendly Dictator," *Carnegie Endowment for International Peace*, July 29, 2002. www.ceip.org.

Mark Permenter, "Commanding Presence," *Uta Magazine Online*, Fall 2002. www.utamagazine.uta.edu.

Joyce Rappaport, "Weekly Quotes," *Canadian Institute for Jewish Research*, 2002. www.isranet.org.

Charles Recknagel and Azam Gorgin, "Afghanistan: Karzai Speaks of Accomplishments, Problems in First Months," *Radio Free Europe*, April 10, 2002. www.rferl.org.

Kathleen T. Rhem, "Franks: A Leader Sure of His Mission and His Troops," *American Forces Information Service News Articles*, January 5, 2002. www.defenselink.mil.

Anthony Spaeth, "Dangerous Ground," *Time Asia*, July 22, 2002. www.time.com.

Barbara Starr, "As Pentagon Burned, Plans for War Took Shape," *CNN*, September 6, 2002. www.cnn.com.

Jeannette Steele, "Army General Tries His Sea Legs," *San Diego Union-Tribune*, December 26, 2001. www.signonsandiego.com.

U.S. Department of State, "Bush Hosts Pakistani president Musharraf at White House," February 13, 2002. http://usinfo.state.gov.

———— "United Against Terrorism," November 7, 2001. www.state.gov.

Matt Ward, "Alumnus Leads U.S. Military Effort," *Shorthorn Online*, October 10, 2001. www.theshorthorn.com.

Ed Warner, "Karzai's Prospects," *Global Security*, December 18, 2002. www.globalsecurity.org.

Washington Post, "The Life of George W. Bush," 1999. www.washingtonpost.com.

David Wastell, "General's Caution Dismays Rumsfeld," *Telegraph*, November 15, 2002. www.telegraph.co.uk.

Rahimullah Yousafsai, "ABC Interview with Osama bin Laden," *Jihad Unspun*, January 1998. www.jihadunspun.net.

Phil Zabriskie, "Where Are the Taliban Now?" *Time*, September 24, 2002. www.time.com.

★ Glossary ★

al-Qaeda: A worldwide terrorist organization headed by Osama bin Laden.

burka: Robe designed to cover a woman's entire body, including the face; a required article of clothing under the Taliban regime.

buzkashi: A violent Afghan sport in which teams of horsemen attempt to toss the headless carcass of a calf into a circle.

Central Command (CENTCOM): One of nine unified combatant commands that control U.S. combat forces around the world.

communism: A system of government in which the state plans and controls the economy; a single, often authoritarian, party holds power, claiming to make progress toward a higher social order in which all goods are equally shared by the people. The Soviet Union was a Communist-led country from 1917 until 1991.

Koran: The sacred book of the Muslims; its contents are reported revelations made to the prophet Muhammad by Allah (God).

loya jirga: Grand council in charge of national decision making in Afghanistan.

madrassas: Islamic religious schools.

mujahideen: Islamic holy warriors.

mullah: An educated Muslim man.

Northern Alliance: A loose association of rebel Afghan leaders who banded together to fight the Taliban.

Sharia: A body of Islamic regulations that governs all parts of life including religious observances, government, and social and private behavior.

shalwar kamees: Loose trousers and tunics worn by Afghan men.

shura: Council.

Taliban: The fundamentalist followers of Mohammad Omar who controlled Afghanistan from 1996 to 2001.

U.S. Special Forces: Units of highly specialized warriors trained to conduct difficult, covert, or unusual missions. In the U.S. military these can include Green Berets, U.S. Army Rangers, Navy SEALS, and others.

warlord: Powerful regional leader who fights to maintain control of his empire.

★ Index ★

★ Picture Credits ★

Cover Photos: Associated Press, AP (background); © Reuters NewMedia Inc./CORBIS (upper left and lower left); © AFP/CORBIS (upper right and lower right)

Associated Press, ALEXANDER SEKRETAREV EST, 71

Associated Press, AL-JAZEERA TV, 24

Associated Press, AP, 14, 16, 30, 35, 37 (top), 39, 44, 49, 51, 53, 54, 55, 59, 70, 74, 79, 83, 88

Associated Press, MBC, 13, 19

© CORBIS SYGMA, 26, 27

Department of Defense photo by Cedric H. Rudisill, 9

Department of Defense photo by Helene C. Stikkel, 81 (top), 81 (bottom), 87

Department of Defense photo by R.D. Ward, 37 (bottom), 58, 64, 66

Department of Defense photo by Sgt. Kevin P. Bell, U.S. Army, 46

Getty Images, 47, 48

Michael Riger/FEMA News Photo, 22

SFC Thomas R. Roberts/ NGB-PASE, 25, 31

U.S. Army photo by Spc. David Marck Jr., 7, 42, 62, 76

★ About the Author ★

Diane Yancey works as a freelance writer in the Pacific Northwest, where she has lived for over twenty years. She writes nonfiction for middle-grade and high school readers and enjoys traveling and collecting old books. Some of her other books include *Leaders of the North and South* (Civil War), *Strategic Battles* (Civil War), and *Life of an American Soldier* (Vietnam War).